# THE
# CAYMAN ISLANDS
## *Dive Guide*

*Text and photographs by* STEPHEN FRINK *and* WILLIAM HARRIGAN

*Editing provided by* Diving Science and Technology Corp. (DSAT)
a corporate affiliate of
Professional Association of Diving Instructors (PADI)

ABBEVILLE PRESS PUBLISHERS
*New York   London   Paris*

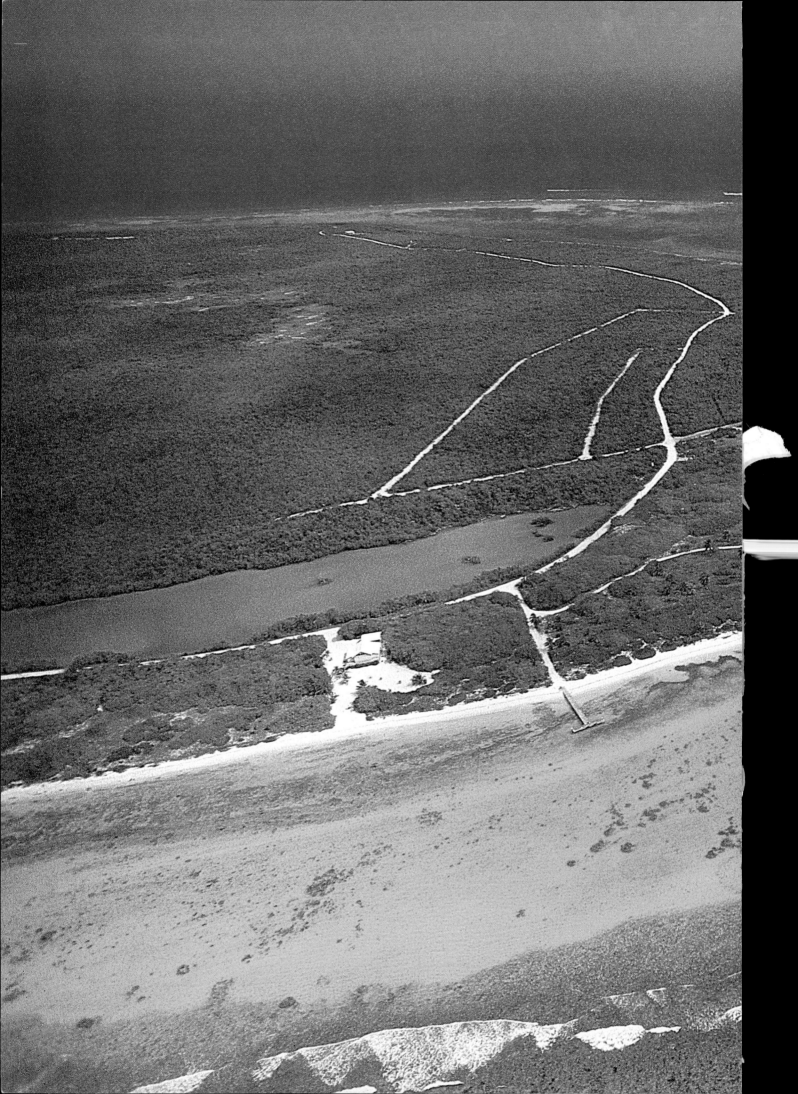

# THE CAYMAN ISLANDS
## *Dive Guide*

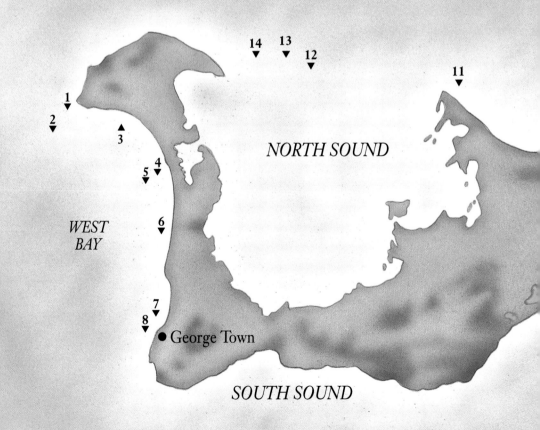

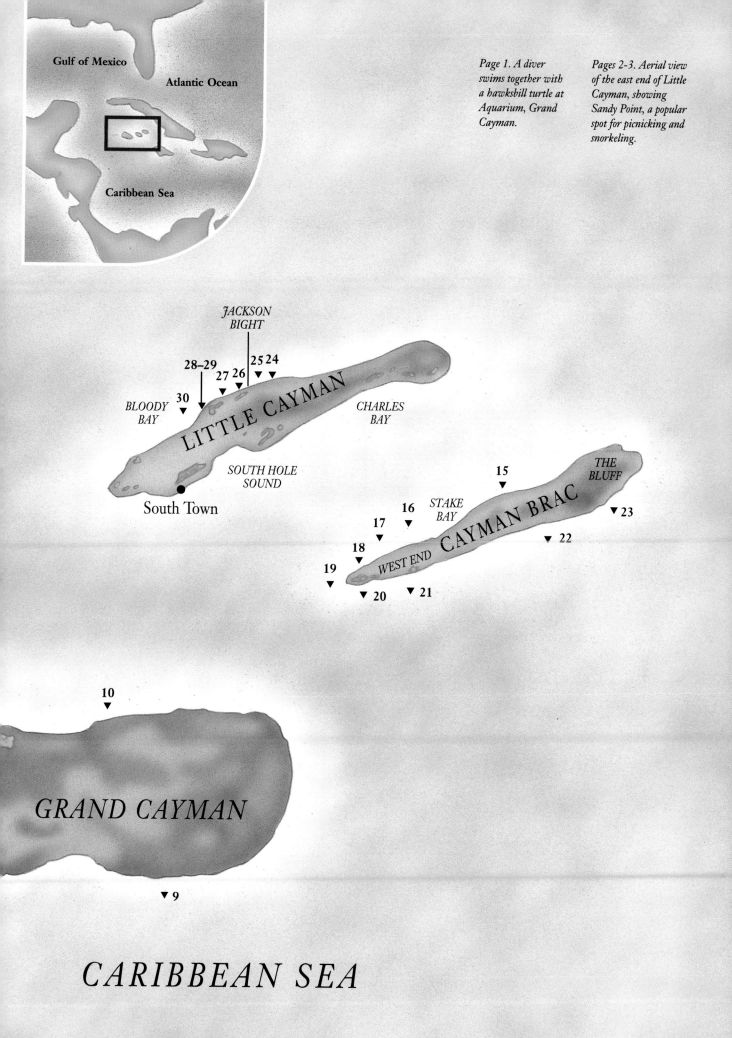

Gulf of Mexico

Atlantic Ocean

Caribbean Sea

*Page 1. A diver swims together with a hawksbill turtle at Aquarium, Grand Cayman.*

*Pages 2-3. Aerial view of the east end of Little Cayman, showing Sandy Point, a popular spot for picnicking and snorkeling.*

*JACKSON BIGHT*

28–29  25 24
27 26
30
*BLOODY BAY*

LITTLE CAYMAN

*CHARLES BAY*

*SOUTH HOLE SOUND*

South Town

15  *THE BLUFF*

16  *STAKE BAY*  ▼ 23
17
18  CAYMAN BRAC  22
19  *WEST END*
20  21

10

GRAND CAYMAN

▼ 9

*CARIBBEAN SEA*

# INTRODUCTION

I f there is any place on earth created just for divers, it must be the Cayman Islands. Geologically, the three islands are uniquely suited for diving, with clear water, vertical walls, shallow coral reefs, and miles of superb sandy beach. Fortunately (for the divers at least) numerous shipwrecks have also come to rest here, some by accident and others by design. Weather and sea conditions are excellent year-round, and the dive sites require typically short boat rides for access.

Historically, these islands remained undeveloped for centuries, as though waiting for a future that was certain to arrive. In the early 1970s, as destination scuba diving first became a viable industry, it was the Cayman Islands that set the standard.

Here were natural resources more than sufficient to attract dive travelers, and a government and private sector

A

B

prescient enough to realize that their underwater world was worth promoting.

Fortunately, the Cayman Islands also realized this massive tourist attraction was worth preserving as well, making marine conservation a national priority far before it became fashionable in other destinations.

Today a full one-third of all tourists to the Cayman Islands arrive specifically for the dive and snorkel attractions. The dive resorts are very diver-friendly, and the dive infrastructure is among the world's most sophisticated and professional. No matter where you choose to dive in the Cayman Islands, you can count on a fascinating underwater world and reliable dive services.

The highest point on Grand Cayman is just 49 feet (14.7 meters), and even the tall bluff of Cayman Brac rises only 140 feet (42 meters), but from a diver's point of view the Cayman Islands are lofty mountaintops, the pinnacle of the recreational dive pantheon. Only small slivers of land actually extend above the surface of the sea, but the islands are the upper reaches of an impressive submarine ridge extending from Belize to Cuban Sierra Maestra, forming the northern edge of the Cayman Trench.

Created by volcanic activity 70 to 50 million years ago, the Caymans are remnants of a prehistoric cataclysm that also created the south coast of Cuba and the central regions of Haiti and Puerto Rico. The nature of the Caymans' geologic origins is significant to divers for a number of reasons.

First, the violent upthrust of the earth's plates created the spectacular vertical walls that ring all three of the islands.

Second, because of its volcanic origins, the porous substrate has no rivers and is covered by very little sediment. This fortunate situation minimizes freshwater runoff and keeps the water extremely clear. Even when the weather brings wind and rain, the visibility tends to stay high and clears quickly.

Third, the islands are well situated to attract marine life. Many large adult

pelagic species arrive from the surrounding deep water, and the shallow sounds inside the reef line provide nursery areas for the many fish and invertebrates that ultimately migrate to the coral reef.

## THE DIVE SITES

There are well over two hundred named dive sites in the Cayman Islands, and many more unmarked and unnamed sites that are visited by various dive operators. Incredibly, in spite of the high level of diving activity over the past three decades in the Caymans, many

areas have yet to be explored. Maybe that's not so surprising when you consider the massive coral reef and drop-off that surrounds all three islands.

The Cayman dive portfolio is so huge and of such high quality, we can only look at a small vignette within the context of this book. The thirty dive sites selected for this book were chosen to represent the range of diving experiences available on Grand Cayman and the Sister Islands.

You'll find your own favorites as you explore the Caymans, from among these sites and many others.

## MARINE ECOLOGY

At the heart of this complex and wonderful submarine world is the tiny coral polyp. The largest of these colonial animals is about the size of the tip of your little finger; most are much smaller. In spite of their diminutive size, coral polyps build miles of massive yet intricate reefs.

Much of the reef-building ability of hard corals is due to their unique symbiotic relationship with tiny algae called zooxanthellae. The zooxanthellae are responsible for the golden brown, yellow,

*A. A green sail interrupts the blue expanse of the sea at Rum Point Beach, North Sound, Grand Cayman.*

*B. The crystal clear waters of Little Cayman are attractive not only to divers.*

*C. Many Cayman reefs are suitable for snorkeling, with coral formations in shallow water. The white tips and golden brown color on the branches of this colony of elkhorn coral, Acropora palmata, indicate a healthy and growing formation.*

or green colors of many corals and contribute significantly to the energy production of the polyps. In the process of photosynthesis, the zooxanthellae use the carbon dioxide and nitrogen waste of the polyp and produce oxygen and nutrients that are in turn used by the polyp. Photosynthesis requires sunlight and is one of the reasons corals only grow in clear and reasonably shallow water.

When the zooxanthellae remove the carbon dioxide and nitrogen, they also act as catalysts in the secretion of calcium carbonate by the polyp. This calcium carbonate forms the skeleton of the reef. Coral polyps obtain the remainder of their nutrients by trapping plankton from

A

the water with their tentacles, which contain stinging cells called nematocysts.

The hard corals' tentacles are normally withdrawn during the day, when plankton are scarce. During this time, polyps rely on the zooxanthellae to produce food. At night, when photosynthesis is not possible and plankton comes up from deeper water, the tentacles extend and the polyps feed actively.

Soft corals, which generally have eight tentacles on each polyp, as opposed to six in hard corals, are found in great numbers on the reef but are not reef builders. Lacking symbiotic zooxanthellae, they form flexible skeletons instead of the hard calcium carbonate skeletons

of the boulder and branching corals. The tentacles of soft corals are normally extended to feed during the day as well as the night.

## MANGROVE FORESTS

The shallow waters of mangroves are not generally visited by Cayman dive operators, but from an ecological standpoint they are vitally linked to the reefs. Coral reefs need clear, warm water in order to survive. They also need water that does not contain too many nutrients, or faster growing organisms like algae will successfully compete with them for space.

B

The plants onshore, particularly the mangroves, are essential in preserving the necessary water quality. Mangroves are uniquely structured to live on the boundary between land and sea. Special adaptations allow them to tolerate salt water, and long roots let them actually grow past the shore and right into the water.

The tangled miles of mangrove roots along the coast stabilize the land and prevent runoff from making the water turbid and overloaded with nutrients. They also provide a protected habitat for many species of fish and invertebrates, particularly during the juvenile phase of the life cycle.

## SEA GRASS

Unlike algae, sea grass actually has roots. It grows underwater, but is much the same as the grass on a lawn. The Cayman reefs, particularly along the north wall of Grand Cayman, benefit from the presence of several species of sea grass, most notably turtle grass and eelgrass. These two grasses often grow in the same area, but can be easily differentiated: turtle grass has flat blades, and eelgrass has round blades.

Sea grasses are incredibly efficient at trapping particles in the water and binding up sediment. The root system can be as long as 3 feet (1 meter), with

*A. Golden branches of elkhorn coral,* Acropora palmata, *can be found on many Cayman reefs. This relatively fast-growing coral can be found in greatest abundance on the shallow reef crests, in the strongest sunlight and highest wave action.*

*B. Multibarreled tube sponges make a colorful foreground on Cemetery Wall, Cayman Brac.*

*C. A school of grunts slides along the wall at Three Fathom Wall, Little Cayman.*

*D. A diver lights the colors of an unusual combination of azure vase sponges,* Callyspongia plicifera, *strawberry vase sponges,* Mycale laxissima, *and a colony of giant star coral,* Montastrea cavernosa, *at Babylon, Grand Cayman.*

*E. Divers can observe southern stingrays at very close quarters at Stingray City.*

*F. This wall at Fantasy Island, Grand Cayman, is rich in life forms, particularly sponges and corals.*

many wandering tendrils that weave the bottom into a thick mat. The blades of grass also trap sediment, giving them a typically fuzzy appearance. This helps keep the water clear for the corals on the reefs. Like other green plants, sea grass employs photosynthesis for its energy needs and releases oxygen, which is also vital to the coral reef ecosystem. As you snorkel or dive near a sea grass bed, you can actually see oxygen released as bubbles. Sea grasses also function as nurseries, providing homes for many of the juveniles of fish and invertebrates that later make their way out to the reef. Finally, sea grasses are an important food source. Herbivores of all types graze regularly on sea grass, including a variety of fish and turtles. Many of the fish that reside on the near shore reefs during the day leave the shelter of the reefs at night to feed on the surrounding sea grass.

The shallow Cayman reefs, located between the deep wall and the islands, are composed of a series of coral ridges and sand channels commonly called "spur and grooves." The ridges are formed by the accumulated calcium carbonate secretions of thousands of years of coral growth. On top of these ridges, living corals are contributing their own tiny amounts of calcium carbonate, or limestone, to the reef each day. The ridges always run perpendicular to the shore, from shallow water to deep water. Knowing how the ridges are oriented makes navigation simple. When swimming parallel to the shore, just count the ridges as you cross them. When swimming perpendicular to the shore, keep track of whether you are going toward shallower or deeper water.

## MARINE PARKS

The Cayman Islands Marine Parks consist of three zones, a Marine Park Zone, an Environmental Zone, and a Replenishment Zone. Examples of all three are established in the waters surrounding Grand Cayman, while Cayman Brac and

Little Cayman have only Marine Park Zones and Replenishment Zones. The Environmental Zone along the eastern shore of North Sound on Grand Cayman has the strictest rules. All in-water activities—anchoring and the taking of any marine life—are prohibited. In addition, there is a 5-MPH (8-KPH) speed limit for boats crossing the area.

The Replenishment Zone has prohibitions against spear guns and taking conch or lobster. Line fishing and anchoring is permitted. Marine Park Zones include much of the West Bay of Grand Cayman, and the north and south walls of Cayman Brac and Little Cayman. Most of the dive sites are in this

C

D

E

F

area. Except for cast nets and line fishing from the shore or beyond the wall, no taking of marine life is permitted. Anchoring is not permitted except for boats less than 60 feet (18 meters), and then only when anchored properly in the sand. Get a copy of the Cayman Islands Marine Park regulations and boundaries at the Port Authority office in George Town. The information is contained in the booklet *Guidelines for the Use of Coastal Waters in the Cayman Islands.*

## WATERSPORTS OPERATORS

Most dive operators in the Caymans are members of the Cayman Island Watersports Operators Association (CIWOA), formed in 1981 to encourage safe and environmentally sound business practices. One of the first projects undertaken by the CIWOA was the installation of mooring buoys to reduce anchor damage on the reefs. Before dive computers, the CIWOA instituted a 100-foot (30-meter) depth limit for sport diving. Some operators have begun to allow computer profiles at greater depths, but you should expect to encounter depth and bottom time limitations on many Cayman dives.

## CAYMAN DIVING

Wall diving is the prime attraction in the Cayman Islands, but there are many dives on shallow reefs and wrecks as well. And, of course, there is Stingray City, one of the most unique and exciting dive encounters in the world—and it's only 12 feet (3.5 meters) deep! The most common dive schedule is a two-tank dive in the morning and a one-tank dive in the afternoon. The second morning dive and the afternoon dive are generally on shallow reefs or wrecks.

A

B

A. Treasure Island Divers boat Gatlin ventures over to the southeast corner of Grand Cayman during a spell of calm weather.

B. A Red Sail Sports instructor conducts a Discover Scuba Diving introductory course in the pool at the Westin on Seven Mile Beach, Grand Cayman.

Some operations also feature two-tank dives in the afternoon. A few operators also run three-tank dive safaris that include two deep dives and a shallow dive. Lunch is normally provided on these trips.

Most boats on Grand Cayman pick up divers either directly from the shore of Seven Mile Beach or from canals or marinas in the North Sound. Only a few docks are available to dive boats along the popular west side of the island. The beach boats commonly dive West Bay sites, which are all within the 6- or 7-mile (10- or 11-kilometer) stretch of water along the west coast. Under certain wind conditions, the south coast or north coast will also be accessible to these boats, but the hull design that makes these vessels ideally suited to a beach pickup also limits their use to calm seas. Boats that operate from the North Sound tend to dive primarily on the North Wall and West Bay, although they are generally capable of going nearly anywhere under the right weather conditions. A relatively small group of dive operators visit the east end of the island, due to the distance from most shops and the generally rougher sea conditions. When the weather cooperates, the East Wall is definitely worth the trip, offering lots of fish and excellent coral and sponge life. Boats on Cayman Brac and Little Cayman not only operate all around their own islands, they frequently cross the short distance between islands. However, off Little Cayman the most frequently dived sites are along Jackson Bight and Bloody Bay Wall, both of which are normally on the lee side of the island. On Cayman Brac most of the diving is concentrated around the west end of the island, providing short run times for the island's two main dive resorts. Trips are sometimes scheduled to the walls along the rugged bluff at the east end of Cayman Brac, but the walls typically begin deeper there. Since it is nearly as easy to cross to Little Cayman as it is to dive the east end

C

D

walls, boats from the Brac often visit Little Cayman rather than dive their own island's more remote reaches.

## RECOMPRESSION CHAMBER

There is a recompression chamber located in George Town, Grand Cayman. A 24-hour-a-day medivac service from Cayman Brac or Little Cayman assures that a quick response to a dive emergency is possible anywhere within these islands. While about 700 treatments have been rendered in the chamber since it was installed in 1972, given the number of divers visiting these islands, the safety record is excellent. Still, careful attention to safe dive profiles and the maximum depth limits imposed by the Cayman Islands Watersports Operators Association should ensure that your Cayman dive holiday will not include a visit to the chamber. Phone 345-949-2989 for more details about the chamber (but hopefully not for reservations).

## GENERAL DIVING CONDITIONS

There is good diving around the entire perimeter of all three islands. However, because the trade winds are usually blowing from the northeast or east, most of the diving occurs on the western ends of the islands, where there is shelter from the wind. The landmass of the islands provides such an efficient lee that many dive sites are in perpetually flat water. Strong currents can be present from time to time, but they are not generally a problem in the Caymans. This is especially true in West Bay, which offers mild surface and subsurface conditions most of the time.

## SHORE DIVING

Most shore diving occurs on the west coast of Grand Cayman, just south of George Town. The reef is very close to shore, and divers can easily reach sites like Eden Rock and Devil's Grotto. There is excellent shore diving just a short walk away from dedicated dive resorts like Sunset House and Coconut Harbor, which makes them especially popular among visiting scuba enthusiasts. Some dive operations may require that you rent tanks from them in order to enter the water from their property.

## BOAT DIVING

The sophisticated level of service provided by dive operators in the Caymans is reflected in their boats. Generally these are well-equipped, well-maintained,

C. A dive boat awaits at its mooring on Cayman Brac.

D. Captain Kevin Dobbs conducts a dive briefing for Fantasy Island aboard Manta, Sunset Divers' luxurious dive cat.

E. Stingray City is one of Grand Cayman's most popular attractions.

F. Red Sail Sports' custom dive boat, a triple-hull, diesel-powered craft with all the modern diver amenities, designed for beach pickups.

G. Sunset harbor tour, George Town, Grand Cayman.

and custom-built for diving. Boats operating primarily in West Bay tend to be catamarans, which are suitable for beach pickups and for the flat water that prevails. Boats operating along the north, south, and east walls are mostly monohulls in the 35- to 45-foot (10- to 14-meter) range, capable of handling rougher sea conditions. Diver capacities of 12 to 24 are common. Amenities generally include freshwater showers, camera rinse barrels, marine heads, drinking water, shaded seating areas, and large swim platforms with long, sturdy dive ladders.

## MOORING BUOYS

Any time an anchor is dropped, there is potential it will fall into coral or drag across the reef. Misplaced anchor chain and line are also potential causes of reef damage. The dive boat captains in the Caymans are very sensitive about protecting their coral reef, and none would intentionally drop the hook in coral. However, the wind could shift during a dive, and with divers down, the captain may not be able to maneuver the boat to avoid potential coral damage. Mooring buoys are a much safer, more environmentally friendly alternative. The mooring buoys used in the Cayman Islands are

white balls that float on the surface, tethered by a line and secured to the seafloor by an eyebolt fastened directly into the bottom. A short line floats on the surface so that the dive boat can simply pull up to the mooring and quickly attach its line to the float. This system not only reduces anchor damage to the coral but is a more efficient way to secure the boat on-site.

About 250 mooring buoys have been installed at dive sites among the three islands. This number changes as new dives are added to the portfolio, moorings are temporarily lost, and sites are temporarily "retired" to allow recovery. Even though mooring buoys mark most of the dive sites discussed in this book,

A

B

C

D

some may be dived as an "anchor drop" either because the mooring ball is presently gone or because the site has never been moored. If an anchor is dropped, rest assured the captain knows how to place the anchor carefully in a sand patch where the chain and line is unlikely to impact coral.

However, if you notice an anchor potentially dragging or apparently ready to damage coral, the captain will appreciate polite notification.

## SCUBA ETIQUETTE

Some special considerations apply to diving in the Cayman Islands due to the popularity of diving here and the fragile nature of coral reefs. Part common sense and part marine park rules, diving etiquette is a set of guidelines for divers that is easy to follow and should not make your diving any less enjoyable.

In fact, following these simple guidelines will ensure that you have the best dive possible and help preserve the reefs for others:

1. Avoid all contact with living coral. No one visiting a palace would tramp through its splendid rose garden; a coral reef should receive the same respect.

The impact of fins, tanks, or knees can crush the septa of coral polyps or remove their protective mucus coating.

F

A. Two scuba divers preparing for shore diving at Grand Cayman

B, D. Grand Cayman dive boats are usually well-equipped and are generally vessels especially built for diving.

C. Divers leaving for shore diving in the northern part of West Bay, Grand Cayman.

E. The photographer completely surrounded by a gang of rays at Stingray City. Divers always have to respect

these friendly animals, even if the rays often get too close.

F. A diver approaching a narrow passage at Babylon, Grand Cayman. You must always control your position carefully in order to avoid damaging sponges and corals.

G. When diving on a wreck, you can have interesting encounters: the wreck of the Oro Verde is home to several large groupers, including this Nassau grouper, Epinephelus striatus.

E

G

The damage caused by one diver is usually not visible, but the cumulative damage from hundreds of divers visiting the same reef year after year becomes obvious. Good buoyancy control will keep you clear of the coral as you swim along the reef.

2. Do not wear gloves on reef dives if possible, to avoid the temptation to touch unnecessarily.

3. Use sandy areas for contact with the bottom.

When you must steady yourself or stop underwater, settle into one of the many sand patches. Sometimes you may need only to put a fin tip or hand down to control your motion. When this

happens, look for sand. However, when you rise off the sand, do so gently. The silt from a clumsy, over-weighted diver rising off the sand can smother the fragile coral polyps and reduce visibility for other divers.

4. Keep all trash aboard your boat. Plastics in particular are a problem because they last so long and can get wrapped around the coral. Most littering is inadvertent—a sandwich wrapper whipped off the side and similar accidents—so extra care is needed on the water. Even biodegradable trash like apple cores and orange peels should not be discarded on the water, if for no other reason than aesthetics. To the person

who comes behind you and sees it floating on the water, it's still just garbage.

5. Respect the marine life. Harassing turtles or other sea life causes unnecessary and life-threatening stress. Enjoy your encounters with them, but do not attempt to ride them or touch them.

## UNDERWATER PHOTOGRAPHY

Some of the most striking underwater photographs taken anywhere in the Caribbean come from the Cayman Islands. Here are some of the reasons :

1. The exceptional clarity of the water minimizes the problem of white particles,

A

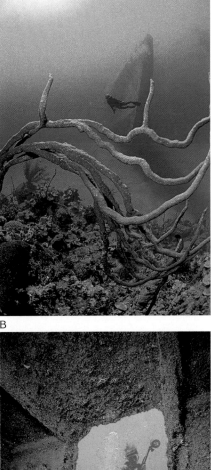

B

A. Wide-angle photography is very good for getting images like this, where the Oro Verde wreck hovers over the bottom, which is rich in marine life.

B. The Cayman Islands offer many advantages for underwater photographers. In addition to clear water, abundant marine life, and interesting wrecks, the islands also have convenient photographic services for film developing, camera rentals, repairs, supplies, and instruction.

known as "backscatter," appearing in the photos.

2. The clear, shallow water allows photographers to make use of strong ambient light for bright backgrounds and an almost three-dimensional look.

3. The Cayman Islands have an enormous variety of marine habitats, from reefs to wrecks to walls, providing countless photo opportunities.

4. High-quality rental cameras and accessories are available at dive shops on all three islands. Quality E-6 slide film and C-41 print film processing is readily available to help quickly evaluate photo progress.

5. The marine life at Stingray City and the Sandbar, including stingrays, moray eels, barracuda, conies, Nassau groupers, yellowtail snappers, and angelfish, is exceptionally tame and can be easily approached for photographs. Other dive sites on all three islands feature marine life that either has been hand-fed or is long accustomed to the benign presence of divers. These fish do

not associate divers with spearfishing, and even normally shy fish like a Nassau grouper will swim right up to a photographer and pose.

6. Photographers are welcome aboard Cayman Islands dive boats, which provide conveniences such as camera tables, rinse barrels, and assistance in handling gear.

7. Customs and Immigrations officials are used to tourists arriving with multiple camera systems, eliminating potential problems entering or exiting the country.

There are so many photographic possibilities on each reef, it may be difficult to decide whether to set up for wide angle, normal, or macro. Here are some tips for what works well in the Caymans:

## WIDE ANGLE

Wide angle is a good choice for the middle of the day, when there is plenty of ambient light to brighten up the background.

C

D

C. Photographers can easily find good subjects, like this green moray eel, Gymnothorax funebris, by looking carefully in the crevices of the reef.

D. A spotted scorpionfish, Scorpaena plumieri, lies camouflaged on the bottom at Eagle Ray Pass, but the photographer's lens has found it.

From about 10 A.M. to 3 P.M. the sun is high in the sky, and more of the sun's rays penetrate the water. During this period you can easily balance the background available light exposure with the foreground strobe exposure.

This is especially true for wide-angle photography on the deeper wrecks. Good sunlight will give you that intense blue background that makes the subject really stand out.

If you happen to be in the Caymans when the weather is not cooperating, wide angle can still be a good choice, as long as you work close. Get in as tight as the lens will allow, and you'll bring back some superb wide-angle shots. Just don't depend too much on the ambient light for your composition or exposure value.

## NORMAL LENS

For the best results, shoot from about 3 feet (1 meter) away, or even closer if your lens and the fish behavior will allow. Move in slowly and carefully to avoid spooking the fish, and you'll be able to capture those head-on, closely packed fish photos that are so appealing.

In addition to schools of fish there are many good single subjects that are the right size for normal-lens underwater photography. Sea turtles, nurse sharks, moray eels, and many coral formations are suitable subjects.

Don't expect to get good pictures of six of your dive buddies or the entire bow of the *Oro Verde* shipwreck with a 35mm lens. You'd have to be too far away to get subjects like this in your viewfinder, and the results will be disappointing. If that's what you want to shoot, rent a wide-angle lens so you can move in closer and still capture a large subject.

## MACRO AND CLOSE-UP

You could jump in the water in the Caymans anytime and anyplace with a macro setup and come back with outstanding photos. Some of the most productive areas, though, are the shallow

E

F

G

E. Thanks to the calm waters, it is not hard to take close-ups of Nassau groupers, Epinephelus striatus.

F. The clear waters of the Caymans let you photograph silver schools of fish like these horse-eye jacks, Caranx latus.

G. The light of the strobes creates silver reflections on the bodies in a school of tarpon, Megalops atlanticus, which gather in groups within the protective culs-de-sac of Tarpon Alley, Grand Cayman.

reefs. Here photographers have plenty of time to search for just the right subject to fit in the limited confines of a macro framer. Grand Cayman reefs like Royal Palms Ledge, Aquarium, and Devil's Grotto are packed with photogenic invertebrates and juvenile fish, while both Cayman Brac and Little Cayman likewise abound in subjects.

Night dives are another excellent time to mount a macro tube or close-up kit. Creatures with vibrant hues and bizarre forms come out at night all over the reefs and on the wrecks, too. In addition, it is easier to coax fish into a wire framer at night than during the day.

There are a few days in the Caymans when the visibility is down and the sun does not cooperate. On days like this,

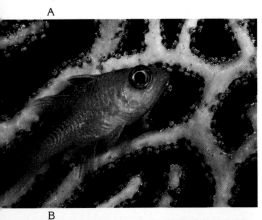

A

B

C

D

*A. Thanks to macro-photography it is possible to admire even the smallest creatures of the sea, like this cardinalfish hiding among the branches of a gorgonian.*

*B. Looking carefully among the bigger coral structures, one can discover infinite life forms. Here a juvenile blenny sits on a coral polyp.*

*C. Even bigger fish, like this Nassau grouper, Epinehelus striatus, can offer a surprise to macro lenses. The image shows the iridescent eye and the opercula of the fish.*

*D. The brilliant red color of a golden zoanthid gives refuge to a tiny yellowline arrow crab, Stenorhynchus seticornis.*

macro is probably the way to go. A strobe or two will provide all the light you need, and the close camera-to-subject distance will make the water look gin-clear again.

## PHOTO ETIQUETTE

Here are a few things to keep in mind when photographing in the Cayman Islands:

1. Getting a good photo is not an excuse for damaging coral. A carefully placed fin tip or finger can let you steady yourself without contacting live coral, and there are plenty of sand pockets where you can stand if you must. However, photographers are expected to have excellent buoyancy control.

2. Harassing the marine life for a photo is also discouraged. Photos of blown-up pufferfish and divers riding turtles show a lack of respect for sea life and the marine environment.

Not everyone on a dive boat appreciates the value or fragility of photo-

graphic equipment. Make sure your camera is not placed on the boat where someone can carelessly damage it. Here are a couple of etiquette tips for non-photographers, too:

1. When you come across a photographer underwater, don't swim in front of the camera, or where your bubbles will rise into the photographer's view.

2. Many photographers will carry more than one camera or strobe, setting them carefully on the bottom when not in use. Expensive cameras are rarely dropped on the bottom and left there by accident, so look around for the photographer before you pick one up, thinking you made the find of the century.

## NIGHT DIVING

When the sun goes down, the reef comes alive. Well, actually a better description might be that sunset is shift-change time on the reef. Creatures that were quiescent during the day become

*E. Night dives make it possible to admire a completely different underwater scenery; even the "actors" change. Here a spider crab, also known as channel spider crab, forages at night.*

active, heading out to forage for food. This includes many invertebrates like crabs and lobster as well as many herbivorous fish.

Other fish that were active during the day, like parrotfish and wrasse, seek shelter within the cracks and crevices of the reef at night.

The most striking difference between daytime and nighttime on the reef, at least for divers, is the color. At night the reef seems to vibrate with reds, oranges,

G

E

H

and yellows that were not visible during the day.

The reason for this apparent change is that at night we are dependent on our dive lights, and everything we illuminate is close by. The light does not travel far enough to suffer the loss of red, orange, and yellow that occurs as sunlight travels through the depths.

All of these factors, plus the inherent mysteries of the nocturnal coral reef, make night diving an exciting activity.

Most Cayman dive operators schedule a night dive at least once a week. Usually additional night dives can be organized whenever four or more divers are interested.

*F. Water is always more nutrient-rich at night, making it easy to see filter feeders at work. The image shows violet feather duster worms,* Bispira brunnea, *on a sponge.*

*G. One of the creatures of the night is the Caribbean reef squid,* Sepioteuthis sepioidea. *The photographer has wisely illuminated this invertebrate, showing the skin and the eye of the animal.*

*H. A shy goldentail moray eel,* Muraena miliaris, *is peeping out of its refuge. At night, moray eels can be found out of their refuges while they look for prey.*

A

B

C

# GRAND CAYMAN

rand Cayman is the largest and most developed of the three Cayman Islands. The relative development level of the three islands is obvious at just a quick glance at the population figures: of the islands' 31,000 residents, 29,500 live on Grand Cayman and only 1,400 live on Cayman Brac. Little Cayman is the most sparsely populated island, with a little more than a 100 permanent residents.

Tourism is huge in the Caymans, with 381,186 air arrivals and an incredible 865,383 cruise ship arrivals in 1997. Grand Cayman receives by far the greatest percentage of general tourism. Tourism officials speculate that about a third of Cayman Islands visitors come specifically for its scuba and snorkel attractions.

Grand Cayman was the island most responsible for the sport diving boom in

D

A. In this aerial view of West Bay, Grand Cayman, you can see the reef and the sandy bottom.

B. The photo shows a small portion of Seven Mile Beach as seen from the balcony of an ocean-view room at the Westin.

C. During dives in Grand Cayman waters one can encounter large animals like this jewfish, Epinephelus itajara.

D. The photographer has found, hidden among the coral, a Caribbean spiny lobster, Panulirus argus. The crustacean, very common in the Cayman waters, waves its antennae against invaders.

the Caribbean in the 1980s—the result of both effective marketing and an extraordinary product.

The circumference of this 22-mile (35-kilometer)-long by 8-mile (13-kilometer)-wide island has nearly 60 miles (100 kilometers) of shoreline well suited to diving. Reefs, wreck, walls, and lots of marine life are the signatures of a Grand Cayman dive adventure.

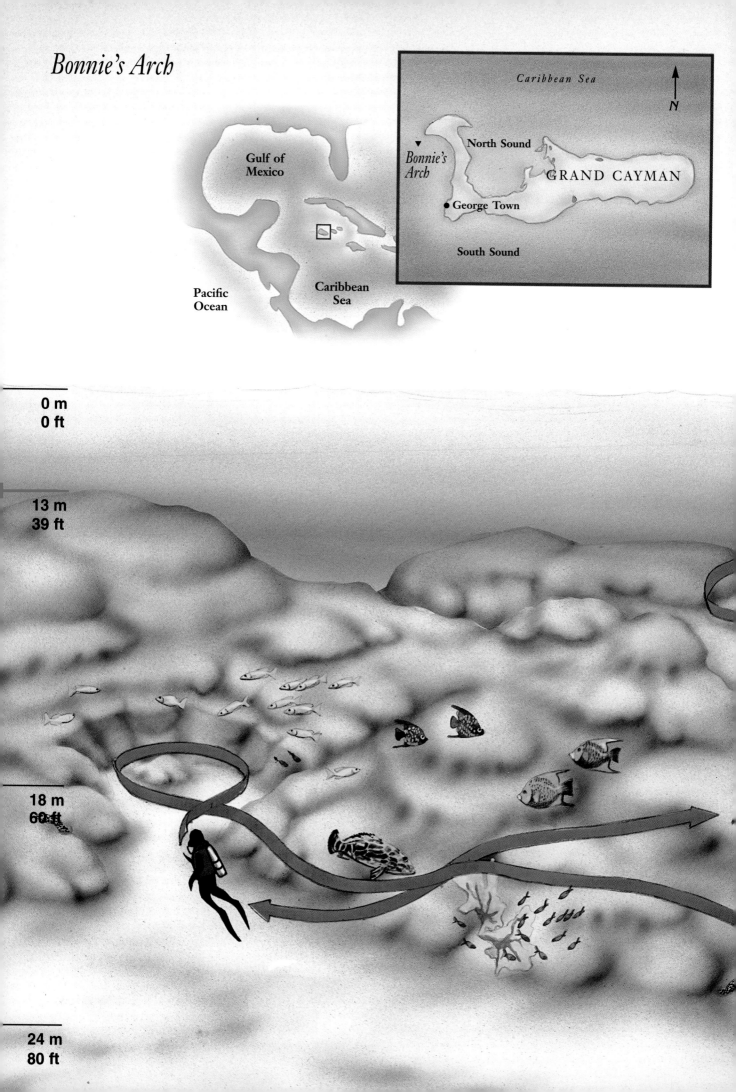

# Bonnie's Arch

Gulf of Mexico

Pacific Ocean

Caribbean Sea

*Caribbean Sea*

*N*

North Sound

*Bonnie's Arch*

GRAND CAYMAN

● George Town

South Sound

0 m
0 ft

13 m
39 ft

18 m
60 ft

24 m
80 ft

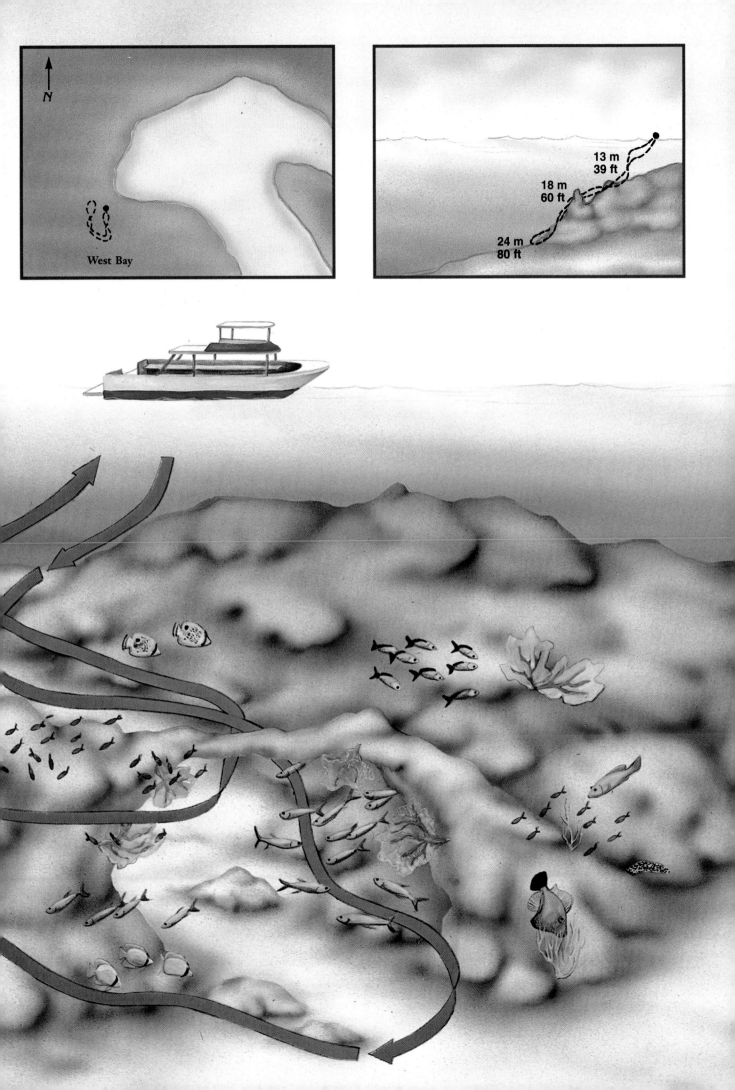

West Bay

N

13 m
39 ft

18 m
60 ft

24 m
80 ft

# Bonnie's Arch

Bonnie's Arch is an example of a great dive unsuited to large numbers of divers visiting at any one time. If you are on a boat with only a half dozen or so divers, then Bonnie's Arch is a must-do. Another way to access Bonnie's Arch is as a shore dive, although because the access is from the rugged ironshore in front of Dolphin Point or Bonnie's Arch Condominiums, shore dives should only be attempted under calm conditions. It is one thing to enter the sea from the ironshore, but quite another to get safely back ashore under surge conditions.

Bonnie's Arch is named for a talented underwater photographer named Bonnie Charles who died in a diving accident on Grand Cayman in the early 1980s. This was one of her favorite dive sites, probably for many of the same reasons it will become one of yours. The underwater seascape here makes it one of the most memorable dive sites on the island. The spur-and-groove coral formations

A

B

C

D

*A, D. Tarpon,* Megalops atlanticus, *are often found beneath the overhang at Bonnie's Arch.*

*B. Close to the reef walls at Bonnie's Arch one can observe schools of silvery fish like these horse-eye jacks,* Caranx latus.

*C. A diver watches a gray angelfish,* Pomacanthus arcuatus, *swim close to a colorful sponge.*

rise from the hardpan at about 20 feet (6 meters). There is a mini-wall that parallels the coast here, dropping from about 40 feet to 70 feet (12 to 21 meters), but the primary attraction of this site is a natural coral archway about 30 feet (9 meters) wide. Normally a large school of silvery tarpon can be found resting in the shelter of the archway. It almost seems they are hiding from the sun in the heat of the day, but I'm sure an ichthyologist will have a more logical explanation for their behavior. For whatever reason, these tarpon have been visiting Bonnie's Arch for decades, but they may not be there when you visit, especially if another dive group has preceded you. While they are fairly tolerant of a slow, careful approach, the entire school will spook at overly aggressive bubble-belching bipeds. A large group of divers will likewise alarm the tarpon, the primary reason the site is appropriate only for small groups or individuals. If the tarpon are not beneath the arch, check along the mini-wall to the north. There is a small indent in the wall face where they sometimes congregate. If divers have chased them from there as well, they will probably stay dispersed until the divers leave, and then they will return to their refuge beneath the arch. A school of horse-eye jacks congregates

*E. Bonnie's Arch is known for its swim-throughs, brilliant colors, and prolific marine life. Here you can see colorful sponge fomations.*

*F. A shy spotted moray eel, Gymnothorax moringa, peeps out of the secure refuge of the reef.*

*G. Divers at Bonnie's Arch often encounter colorful animals like this rock beauty, Holocanthus tricolor.*

*H. Sponges provide habitat for a multitude of sea creatures, from anemones to reef fish.*

there as well, so if silvery fish is your objective, Bonnie's Arch is a good place to visit. During the summer and early fall, schools of tiny silversides are also often present, swirling constantly near the protection of the ledges and crevices. Angelfish are common here as well, and because they are so accustomed to divers, they seem to willingly pose at any opportunity.

The reef face is rich with cleaning stations, so shots of tiger groupers with their mouths wide open for cleaning gobies are fairly attainable. Cleaning stations are often located near conspicuous formations, so the numerous large

barrel sponges and colonies of giant star coral at Bonnie's Arch are good places to watch for cleaning activity.

A word of caution about the arch itself. The gorgonia and sponge life used to be more dense and vibrant on the underside of the arch, but decades of diver contact and exhaust bubbles have taken their toll. If you didn't see the arch twenty years ago, you won't know what you've missed, but even though you'll still appreciate the site for

its beauty, something is lost—even our bubbles leave their mark. Left to themselves, the filter feeders will recolonize the arch, but only if divers allow the embryonic sponge and coral to attach and grow.

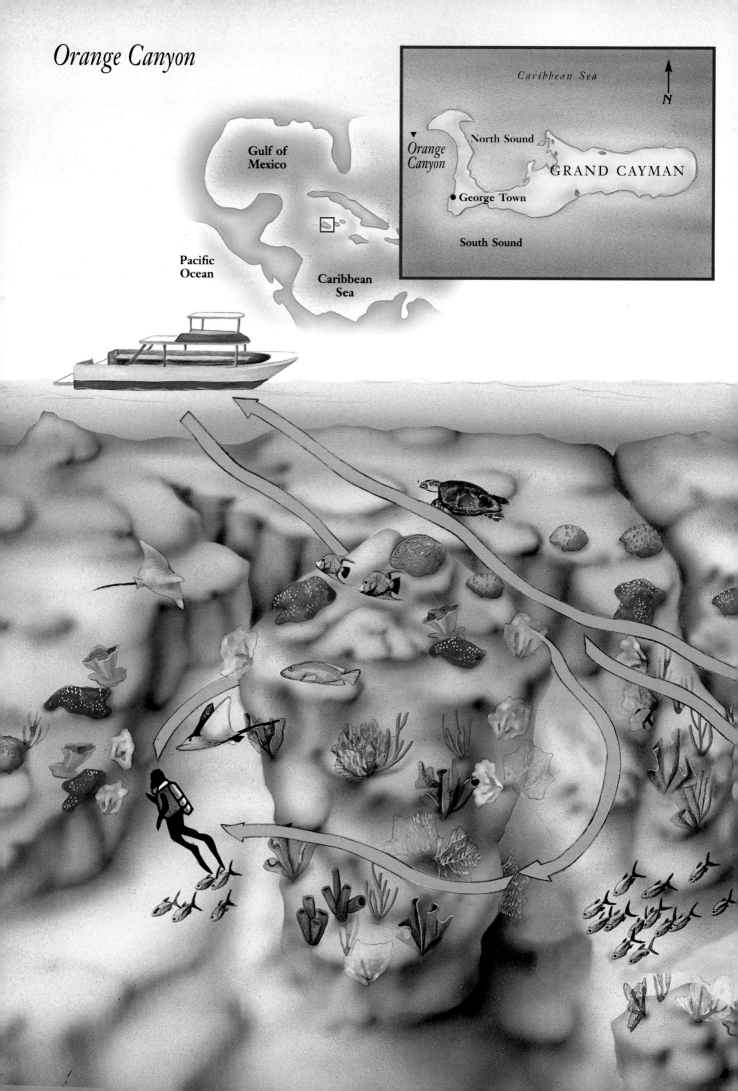

Orange Canyon

Gulf of
Mexico

Pacific
Ocean

Caribbean
Sea

Caribbean Sea

N

Orange
Canyon

North Sound

GRAND CAYMAN

George Town

South Sound

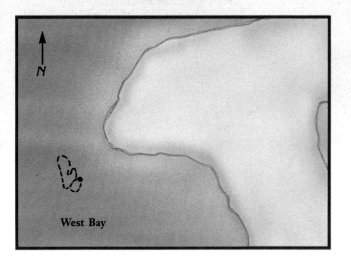

West Bay

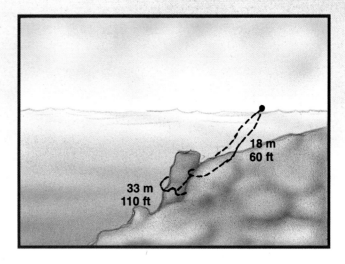

33 m
110 ft

18 m
60 ft

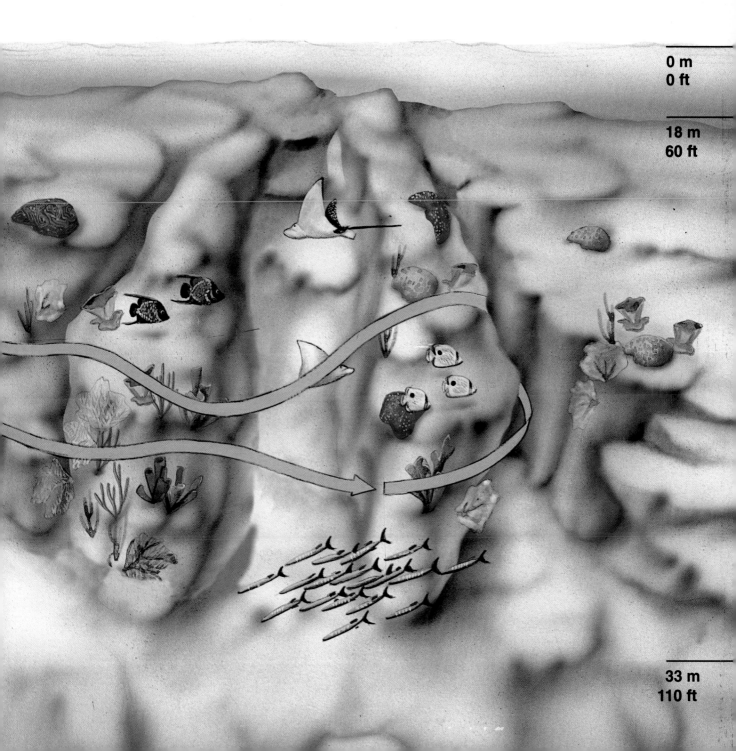

0 m
0 ft

18 m
60 ft

33 m
110 ft

# Orange Canyon

Orange elephant-ear sponges provide the orange in Orange Canyon, growing in abundance along the face of the wall and the deeply cut sides of the canyon. Other sponge species add additional colors to the scene. Red finger sponges, azure vase sponges, and green tube sponges are all

*A. The photograph shows how large sponges can get at Orange Canyon.*

*B. A diver examines a section of the Orange Canyon wall covered with a variety of sponges and coral.*

found in abundance here. Several colonies of giant star coral grow in the less common fluorescent orange form at Orange Canyon, as if the green coloration is too dull for the competition.

This site is located on the steepest and deepest section of the West Bay wall. Actually, it is the promontory that lies within the canyon that first attracts divers, rather than the canyon itself. Located slightly west of the mooring, this is where you first encounter the top

of the wall as you descend. The face of the wall is undercut in many areas, forming interesting profiles that provide excellent habitat for the delicate black corals and sponges that need protection from currents. By contrast the sections of the wall that jut outward are crowded with deep-water gorgonians, a hardy species that thrives in places where strong currents bring abundant food. They grow as large as 5 feet (1.5 meters) in diameter, with thick brown or dark red

*C. Deep-water gorgonians and orange elephant-ear sponges compete for space along a coral ridge at Orange Canyon.*

*D. The diver admires a large elephant-ear sponge,* Agelas clathrodes, *surrounded by deep-water gorgonians at Orange Canyon.*

E

F

G

*E. The artificial lights exalt the brilliant color of a large orange elephant-ear sponge, one of the colorful sponges that give Orange Canyon its name.*

*F. Tube, finger, and encrusting sponges also contribute to the bright splashes of orange and red.*

*G. Although seldom seen during the day, spider crabs can often be observed at night when they come out to feed on algae attached to the reef.*

*H. Many of the crevices in the coral walls at Orange Canyon are filled with schools of silversides, especially during the late summer months.*

branches and light colored polyps. Their bases are often obscured by thick growths of elephant-ear and other encrusting sponges. These clusters of coral and sponge provide protection and food for a wide variety of marine creatures, from tiny invertebrates to large reef fish. Any of these in Orange Canyon are worth a long look, whether you are just admiring the reef or searching for the perfect backdrop for a wide-angle photograph.

The base of the main promontory is cut by a swim-through with a fairly

H

narrow opening. There is sufficient room to pass through with care, but please be mindful of the damage careless kicks cause. Swimming up either side of the coral wall, you will see deeply undercut areas filled with marine life, including a large cul-de-sac that is home to thousands of silversides in the summer. Divers often see hawksbill and green turtles at Orange Canyon, as well as spotted eagle rays and several grouper species. Other fish frequently encountered here include spotted eels, French angelfish, queen angelfish, stoplight parrotfish, trumpet-fish, rock beauties and Creole wrasse. Orange Canyon is at the northern end of West Bay. Visibility is normally excel-lent, in the 80- to 120-foot (24- to 36-meter) range. There is usually a current present, although it doesn't tend to be exceptionally strong.

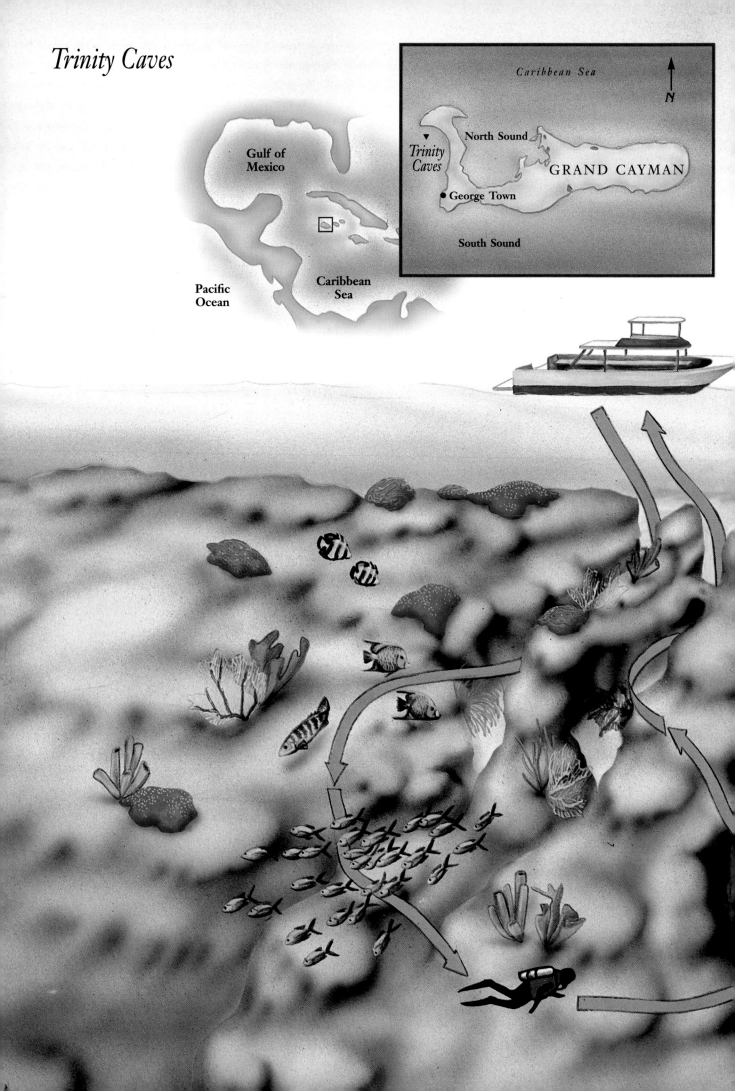

# Trinity Caves

Gulf of
Mexico

Pacific
Ocean

Caribbean
Sea

Caribbean Sea

N

Trinity
Caves

North Sound

GRAND CAYMAN

George Town

South Sound

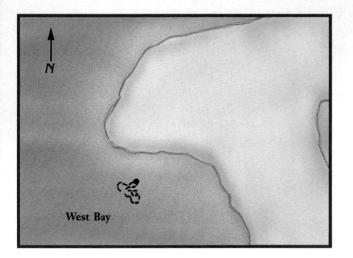

N

West Bay

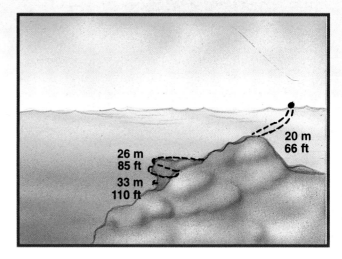

20 m
66 ft

26 m
85 ft

33 m
110 ft

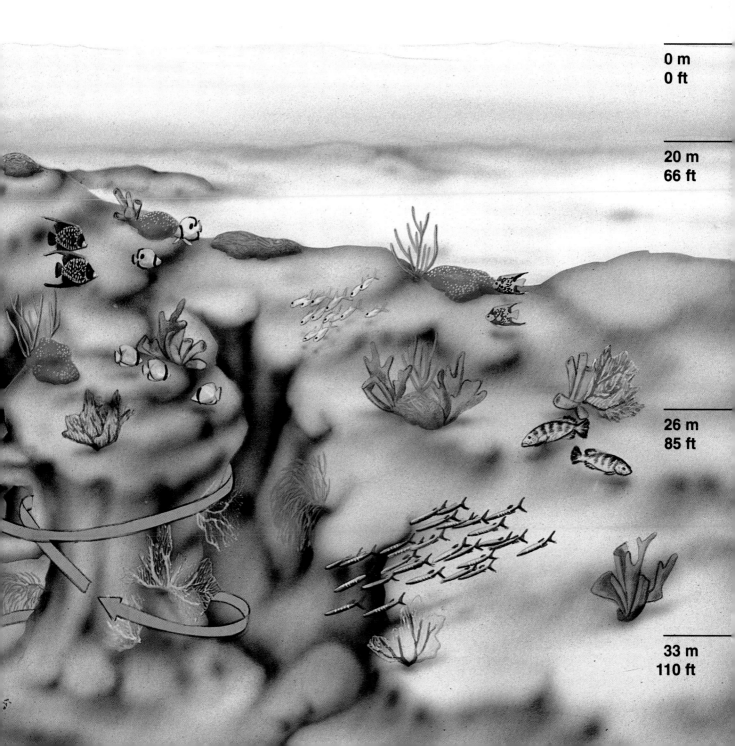

0 m
0 ft

20 m
66 ft

26 m
85 ft

33 m
110 ft

A

# Trinity Caves

There is a series of extraordinary wall dives along the southern end of the West Wall, including sites like Orange Canyon, Big Tunnel, and Trinity Caves. These are remarkable not only for their dimension and decoration, but also because they have been icons of Cayman diving for twenty-five years. Despite the tens of thousands of divers that have visited these sites, they remain compelling and inspirational.

B

D

C

A. A diver swims past a brightly colored orange elephant-ear sponge at Trinity.

B. Sponges of every color and shape decorate the wall at Trinity.

C. Macrophotography lets divers discover the denizens of a small but colorful world, like this banded coral shrimp, Stenopus hispidus, at Trinity.

D. A diver examines the large soft coral colonies at Trinity, wearing a Dive Link system to communicate with his dive partner.

The primary coral growth at Trinity Caves begins at a depth of about 45 feet (13.5 meters). The concentrations of star coral and other boulder corals build up here and cascade gradually seaward.

If you look carefully at the star coral heads here, you can see the full range of growth patterns exhibited by this primary reef-building species. In the shallower area, the heads are tall and well shaped. In deeper water they form knobs to increase their surface area for more light absorption. In the deepest water, they flatten out into plates for maximum surface area. A series of gullies and chimneys offers a convoluted

E

F

G

H

*E. This diver examines a branching red sponge at Trinity.*

*F. A fairy basslet,* Gramma loreto, *swims near a colony of giant star coral,* Montastrea cavernosa.

*G. Divers stop to admire a brightly colored orange elephant-ear sponge at Trinity.*

*H. A juvenile spotted drum,* Equetus punctatus, *finds shelter within the sponges and corals at Trinity.*

route to the vertical wall face.

The overhangs and swim-throughs are the primary attraction of Trinity Caves due to their lush decoration, although the angelfish and tiger groupers commonly seen here add fascination to the dive. Black coral and gorgonia abound, while orange elephant-ear and yellow tube sponges vie for the photographer's attention. The contrast of the vibrant primary colors of the sponge with the cobalt blue of the deep water is an unforgettable image replicated daily at Trinity Caves.

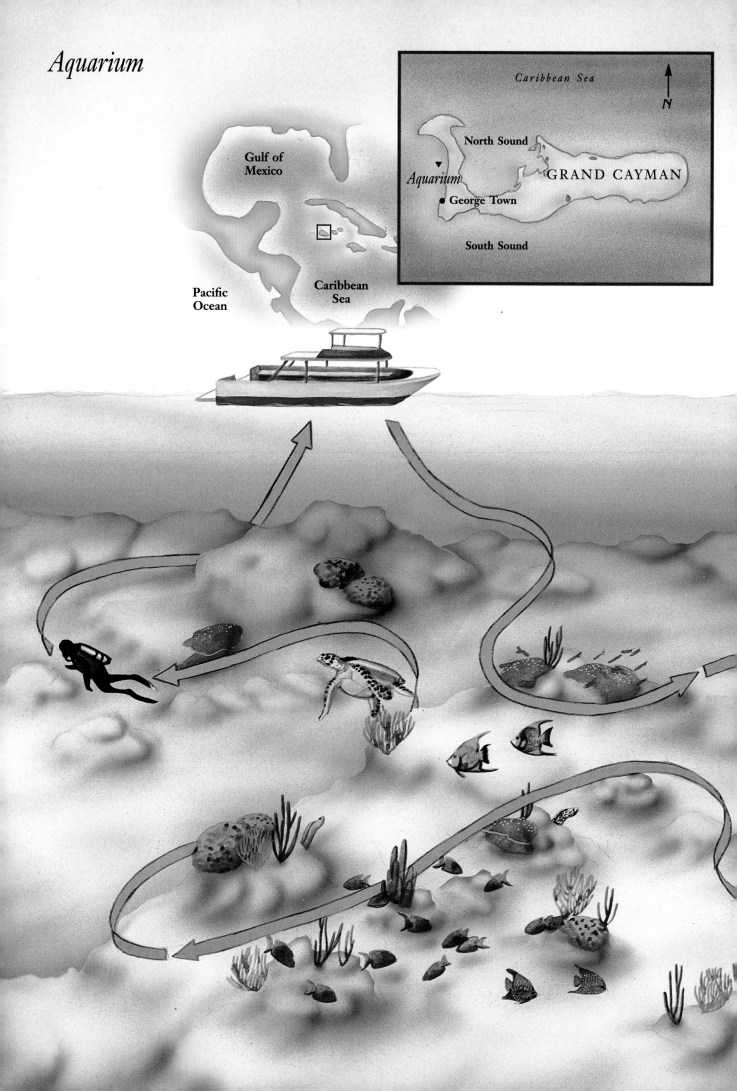

Aquarium

Gulf of
Mexico

Pacific
Ocean

Caribbean
Sea

Caribbean Sea

N

North Sound

*Aquarium*

GRAND CAYMAN

George Town

South Sound

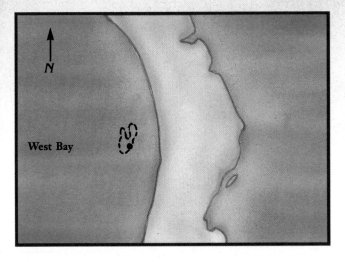

West Bay

N

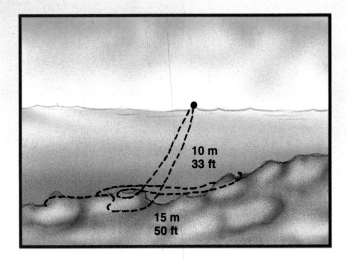

10 m
33 ft

15 m
50 ft

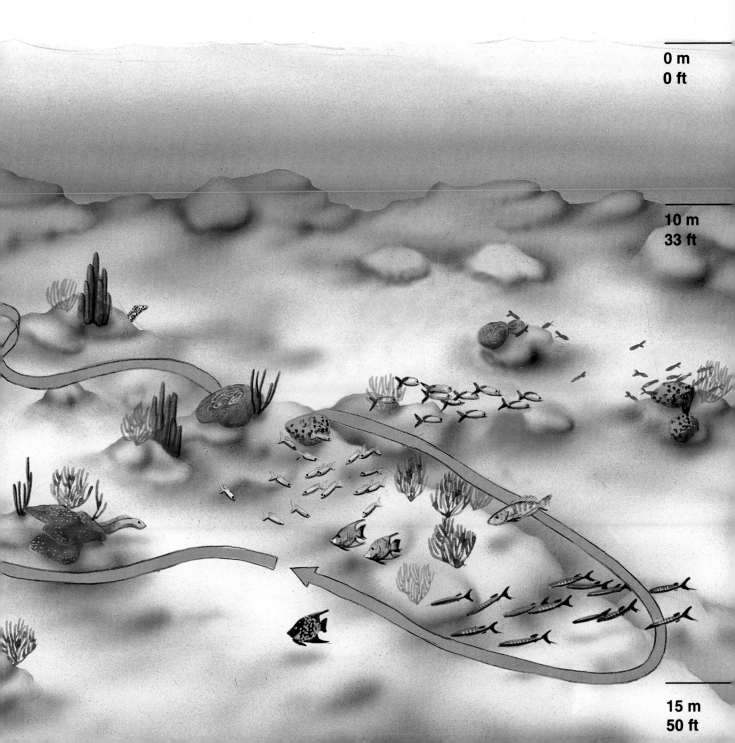

0 m
0 ft

10 m
33 ft

15 m
50 ft

# Aquarium

Any diver interested in tropical fish, whether captured on film or merely observed, will find Aquarium aptly named and appealing. This shallow reef lies in 30 to 45 feet (9 to 13.5 meters) of water, with spur-and-groove formations sloping gently seaward. A sand plain at about 50 feet (15 meters) is punctuated by high-profile coral, like outlying suburbs to the main reef's metropolis. Several kinds of hard coral

comprise the reef, including star, brain, and even pristine stands of pillar coral. The hard coral concentration is such that good buoyancy control is a must to avoid collision, especially when pursuing one of the many photogenic tropicals with an eye glued to the viewfinder. Pillar coral is particularly susceptible to damage due to its tall, narrow columns. Unlike other hard corals, pillar coral often feeds during the day, so its polyps are extended and more easily injured by a careless bump.

Angelfish are especially abundant here, with French and gray angelfish the most common. Queen angelfish will be likely sighted as well, but the

A. *A diver swimming together with a hawksbill turtle at Aquarium.*

B. *Dives at Aquarium can offer interesting encounters like this with a great barracuda,* Sphyraena barracuda.

C. *A school of densely packed sailor's choice grunts,* Haemulon parrai, *can be observed at Aquarium.*

D. *This green moray eel,* Gymnothorax funebris, *is a typical inhabitant at Aquarium.*

E. *A pair of French angelfish,* Pomacanthus paru, *cruise the reef at Aquarium. This dive site is named for the wide variety of reef fish species found there.*

F. *A school of blue tang,* Acanthurus coeruleus, *swarms over the reef at Aquarium, pausing frequently to munch on patches of algae.*

G. *Swimming close to coral formations makes it possible to meet colorful fish like this foureye butterflyfish,* Chaetodon capistratus.

H. *A slender filefish,* Monacanthus tucken, *seeks concealment in the branches of a soft coral at Aquarium.*

I. *Caribbean spiny lobsters,* Panulirus argus, *look for protection beneath a ledge at Aquarium.*

blue angelfish remains elusive even here. Moray eels can be found within the coral crevices, and whitespotted filefish are often seen in pairs here. This is a good site to bring a waterproof fish identification slate and just observe. The areas beneath coral ledges and between heads are good places to look for fish. Brilliant purple-and-yellow fairy basslets, striped harlequin bass and vivid tobaccofish can all be seen in these out-of-the-way spaces at Aquarium.

Even the sandy patches between coral heads are habitat for many fish. Small holes in the sand harbor fish like

bridled gobies, yellowhead jawfish, and sand tilefish. You'll be amazed at the number of different species you'll see on just a single dive.

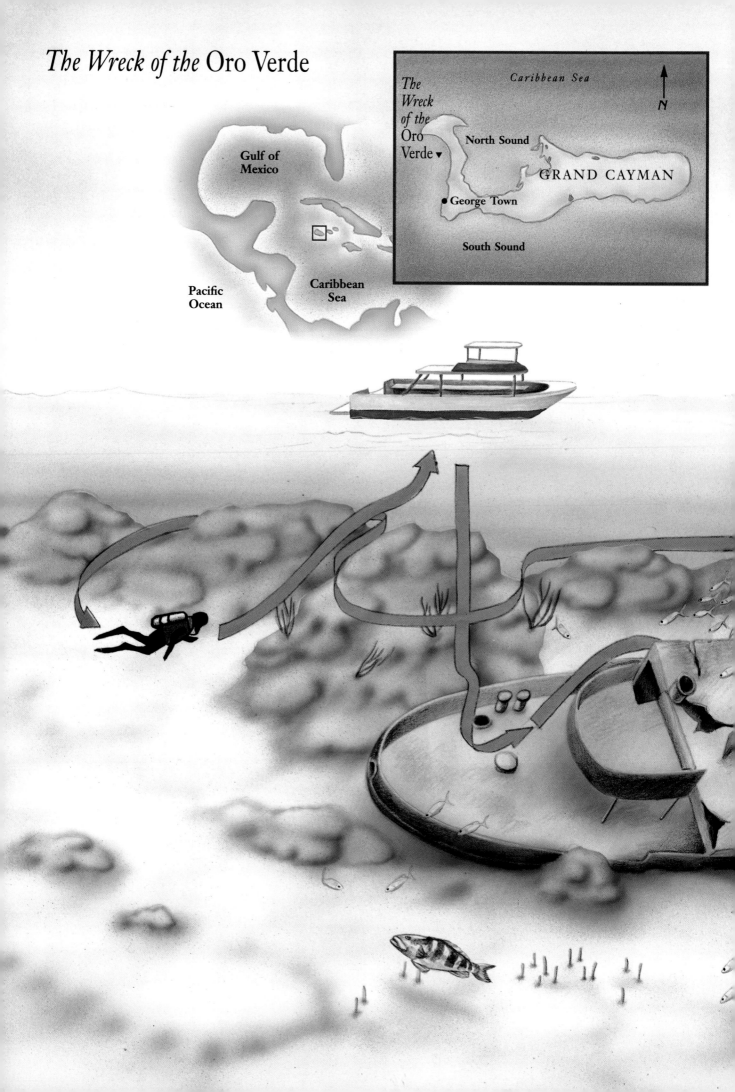

# The Wreck of the Oro Verde

The Wreck of the Oro Verde ▼

Caribbean Sea

N

North Sound

GRAND CAYMAN

● George Town

South Sound

Gulf of Mexico

Pacific Ocean

Caribbean Sea

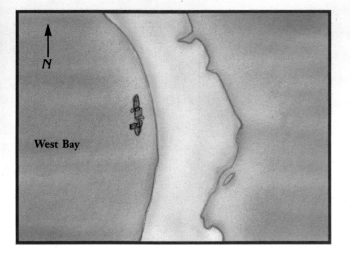

West Bay

N

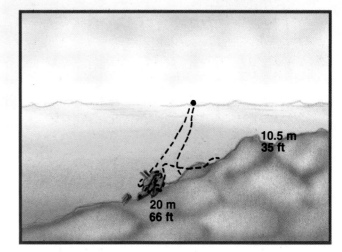

10.5 m
35 ft

20 m
66 ft

0 m
0 ft

10.5 m
35 ft

20 m
66 ft

# The Wreck of the Oro Verde

The 189-foot (57-meter) freighter *Oro Verde* was sunk in 1980 by a coalition of Grand Cayman dive operators. A series of severe storms have twisted the wreck apart, leaving only the bow section intact. Amidships, the hull is scattered on the sand, with the engine plainly visible and large metal plates

heaped haphazardly on the bottom. The propeller has been mangled and detached from the ship and is jammed between the hull and the reef. Larger pieces of the stern remain intact; an anchor and chain lie on the sand off the stern. There are two moorings attached to the *Oro Verde*, one on the bow and one on the stern. The vessel lies on its starboard side, with the keel wedged against the reef and the deck facing a broad sandy plain filled with garden eels.

Despite its years on the bottom, the *Oro Verde* is sparsely covered with encrusting marine organisms. It attracts lots of fish, though, and several large animals have made themselves at home within the metal plates. A large dog snapper often follows divers around the wreck, casting a baleful yellow eye at their explorations. Two green moray eels are usually found within the wreck, often in the deepest part of the center section. A number of tiger groupers hang out in their favorite spots in the

*A. The vessel in this photograph of the wreck of the* Oro Verde *is well preserved; in fact the image is old and shows the wreck just after it was sunk.*

*B. A diver looks at the bow of the* Oro Verde.

*C. This photograph shows the* Oro Verde *wreck in good condition. Due to the relatively shallow position, the vessel was damaged by storms.*

D

can sometimes be found by following their trails in the sand. Conditions here are nearly always calm, with little or no current. The reef slopes gently upward from the wreck toward land, with alternating coral ridges and narrow sand channels. The reef is somewhat sparse, but it is a good location for macrophotography, especially on night dives. The wreck itself only rises perhaps 15 feet (4.5 meters) from the bottom. Visibility is normally 70 to 100 feet (26 to 30 meters), with blue or blue-green water.

*F. A diver approaches the damaged sections of the* Oro Verde.

*G. A diver peers through the stern porthole of the* Oro Verde.

F

E

G

*D. Large animals like this jewfish,* Epinephelus itajara, *have been sighted periodically on the wreck of the* Oro Verde.

*E. The wreck of the* Oro Verde *is home to several fish, including silversides, which reflect light among the metal structures.*

hull, mouths open as a team of gobies industriously cleans them of parasites. Clearly the fish have been fed here; to open a pack of squid or ballyhoo on the wreck of the *Oro Verde* will invite aggressive attention from the resident yellowtail snapper. The sand plain on which the *Oro Verde* rests is about 60 feet (18 meters) deep. In addition to the multitude of garden eels, southern stingrays can usually be found searching the sand for their favorite invertebrates. Single-shelled molluscs like conch and triton

# Royal Palms Ledge

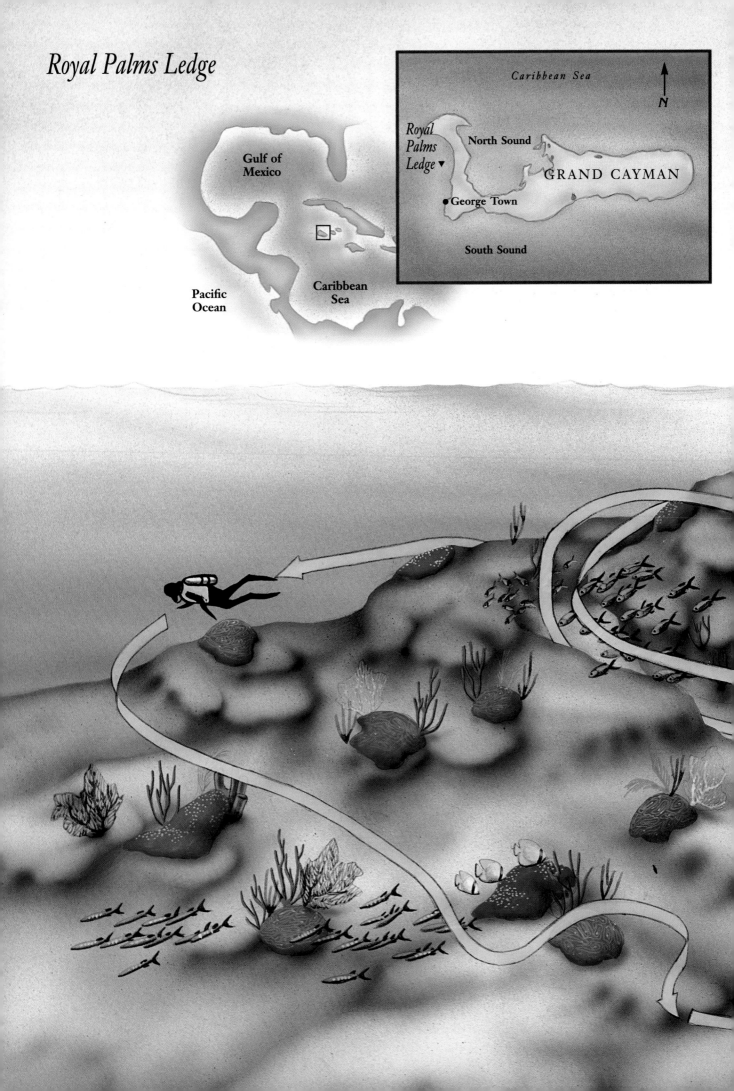

Gulf of Mexico

Pacific Ocean

Caribbean Sea

Caribbean Sea

*Royal Palms Ledge* ▾

North Sound

GRAND CAYMAN

N

● George Town

South Sound

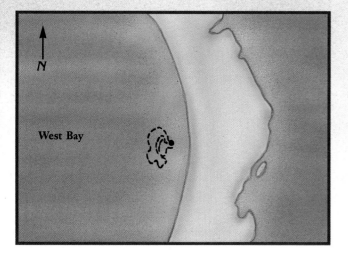

West Bay

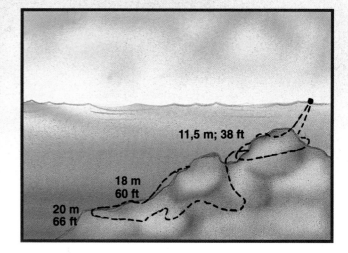

11,5 m; 38 ft

18 m
60 ft

20 m
66 ft

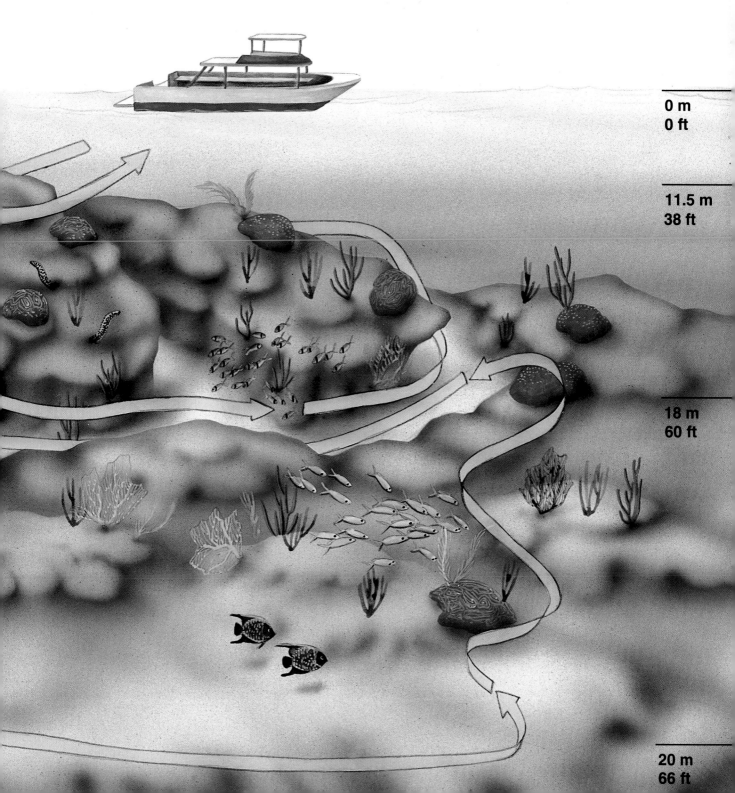

0 m
0 ft

11.5 m
38 ft

18 m
60 ft

20 m
66 ft

# Royal Palms Ledge

This West Bay dive site features an unusual horseshoe-shaped ledge that is deeply undercut around most of its base. Named for the Royal Palms Hotel, lost to fire in 1987, the ledge is a popular site for both day and night dives.

The shallow end of the formation is about 35 feet (10.5 meters) deep, and it slopes downward gradually until it reaches about 55 feet (16.5 meters) at the bend. The underside of the cut is covered with encrusting sponges as well as a tangle of finger sponges. At night the sides of the ledge are a good place to find orange ball corallimorphs and slipper lobsters.

The sand on the base of the ledge and the ledge itself is actually a coral spur and groove that curves around on itself rather than running perpendicular to the shore as most spurs do.

Good buoyancy control is necessary when swimming beneath the edge of the cut. If you are too buoyant, you will touch the wall; if you are stirring up the sand with your fins, you are too negative.

The coral at Royal Palms Ledge is a mix of hard and soft corals. Common

C

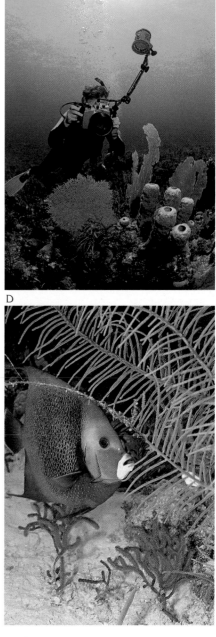

A

B

D

A. A diver examines the spreading branches of a deep-water gorgonian, Iciligorgia schrammi, *beneath the overhang at Royal Palms Ledge.*

B. A coney, Cephalopholis fulvus, *shows off its brilliant golden-phase colors at night on Royal Palms Ledge.*

C. Wide-angle photo opportunities are abundant at Royal Palms Ledge, but this reef is a favorite for macrophotography, too.

D. Gray angelfish, Pomacanthus arcuatus, *are commonly encountered at Royal Palms Ledge.*

gorgonia, sea plumes, and sea rods are all present, filling in the spaces between medium-sized mounds of star, giant star, and brain coral.

An extraordinary number of small fish and invertebrates inhabit the crannies in the corals, making this site a favorite with macrophotographers.

Squirrelfish, banded butterflyfish, blackbar soldierfish, and blueheaded wrasse are among the more abundant reef fish species here. Common invertebrates include flamingo tongues, arrow crabs, scarlet fileclams, bristleworms, and banded coral shrimp.

Visibility is generally between 50 and 70 feet (26 and 30 meters).

G

E

H

F

I

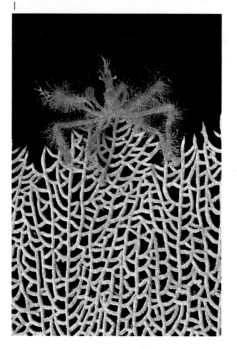

E. The photographer has found a spiny lobster, Panulirus argus, *hidden in the reef on Royal Palms Ledge.*

F. *A yellowhead jawfish,* Opistognathus aurifrons, *seems to observe the camera from its lair in the sand at Royal Palms Ledge.*

G. *Tiny but colorful fairy basslets,* Gramma loreto, *are plentiful at Royal Palms Ledge. They are frequently seen* beneath coral ledges, swimming vertically or upside down as they orient themselves to the shape of the coral rather than the surface of the water.

H. *The photographer has discovered this foureye butterflyfish,* Chaetodon capistratus, *at night on Royal Palms Ledge.*

I. *This neck crab,* Podochela sp., *lies on a gorgonia at night on Royal Palms Ledge.*

# The Wreck of the Balboa

*Caribbean Sea*

N

*The Wreck of the Balboa* ▼

North Sound

GRAND CAYMAN

● George Town

South Sound

Gulf of
Mexico

Pacific
Ocean

Caribbean
Sea

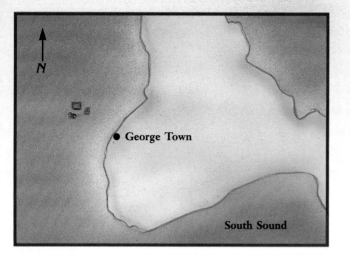

N

● George Town

South Sound

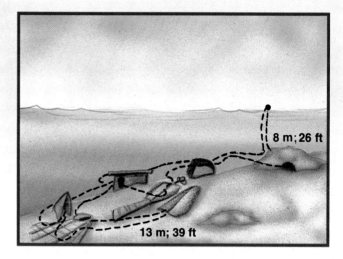

8 m; 26 ft

13 m; 39 ft

0 m
0 ft

8 m
26 ft

13 m; 39 ft

# The Wreck of the Balboa

Located only 200 yards (180 meters) from the main pier in George Town, the wreck of the *Balboa* is one of Grand Cayman's most popular night dives.

The *Balboa* was a 375-foot (112-meter) freighter used to haul lumber. The 1932 hurricane that ravaged the Caymans caught her unprepared in the harbor, and she sank in shallow water.

On several different occasions the hull was intentionally blown apart to clear the harbor for safe navigation. Today all that remains is a line of metal pieces, including a section of the boiler room, the propeller, and a piece of the stern section of the hull.

The engine block can be seen amid the wreckage near the propeller. The prop itself is easy to find, sticking up prominently from the section of hull to which it is still attached. Beyond the prop, the very stern of the ship can also be found relatively intact.

At night the wreckage is fertile ground for macrophotographers. The ship provides excellent habitat for thousands of marine invertebrates, including a variety of crabs, brittle stars, octopuses, anemones, and nudibranchs.

This is a good place to find orange ball corallimorphs, but take care not to shine your dive light directly on them, since they are sensitive to light and will quickly retract into their stalk. If that happens, you'll miss your photo, and the corallimorph will be stressed by wasted energy and missed feeding opportunities.

Many small fishes, like gobies and blennies, also live in or around the wreckage of the *Balboa*. Quite often fish can be found in male and female pairs on the wreck. Whitespotted filefish, for instance, browse together as they feed, as do foureye butterflyfish, banded butterflyfish, and French angelfish.

*A. A diver explores the inner sections of the wreck of the Balboa, Grand Cayman. The vessel is situated at a short distance, only 200 yards (180 meters) from the main pier in George Town.*

*B. The freighter is a very popular dive spot at Grand Cayman. Inside the Balboa you can see many life forms, including colorful sponges.*

*C. Diving inside wrecks is recommended only for expert divers.*

*D. The Balboa sank in 1932 after a violent hurricane that caught the ship unprepared in the harbor.*

*E. A diver examines the propeller of the wreck of the Balboa.*

The metal plates provide food and habitat for many juvenile fish as well, especially angelfish, parrotfish and jacks. It takes patience to spot these little fish because they tend to stay beneath the protection of the metal plates, darting quickly out and returning again.

Depths vary from about 25 to 40 feet (7.5 to 12 meters). Because of its proximity to the harbor, visibility is generally lower here than other sites on Grand Cayman, usually in the range of 30 to 60 feet (9 to 18 meters).

Currents are normally slight. Due to the extensive commercial ship traffic, permission of the harbormaster is required before diving the *Balboa*.

*F. The diver approaches the Balboa, one of Grand Cayman's popular shallow wrecks. Night dives on the Balboa are quite common.*

*G. Night dives offer the possibility for many interesting encounters, like this Caribbean reef octopus, Octopus briareus.*

*H. These bristle-worms, Hermodice caruncalata, can be observed on the wreck of the Balboa.*

*I. The metal plates of the Balboa, as well as the surrounding sandy area, provide habitat for many fish like this lizardfish, Synodus saurus.*

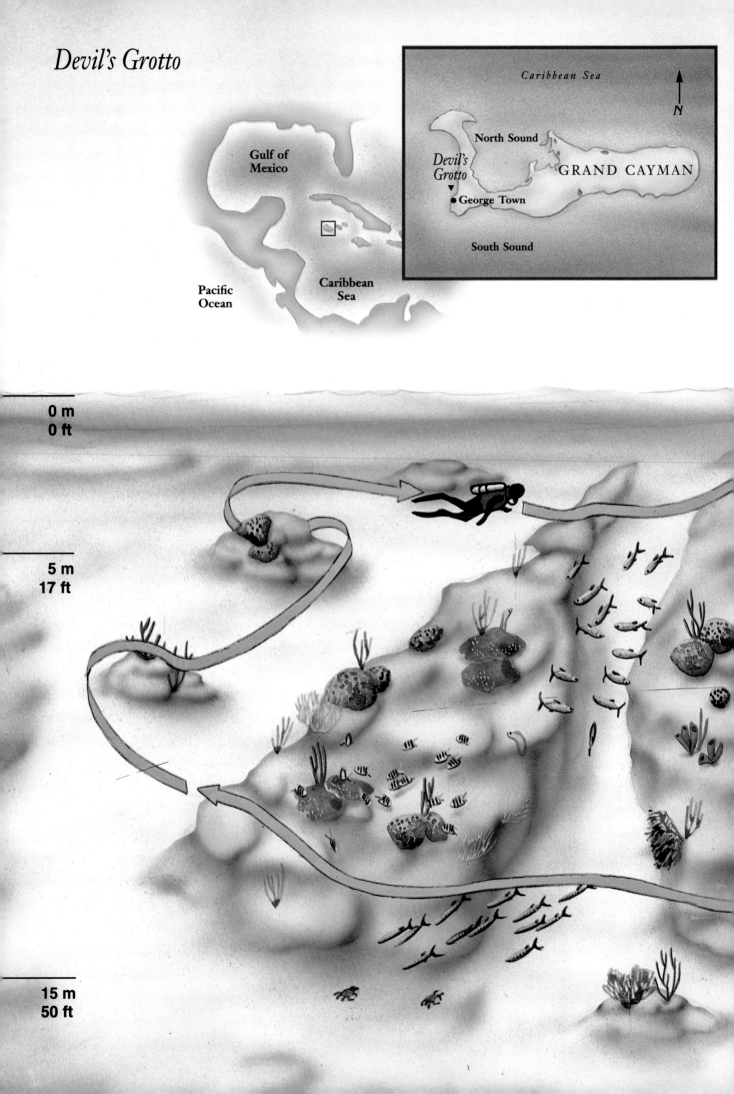

Devil's Grotto

Gulf of
Mexico

Caribbean Sea

North Sound

Devil's
Grotto

GRAND CAYMAN

George Town

Pacific
Ocean

Caribbean
Sea

South Sound

N

0 m
0 ft

5 m
17 ft

15 m
50 ft

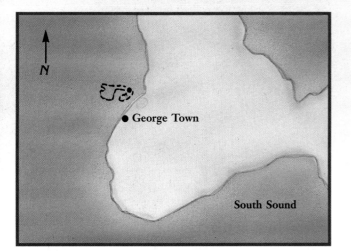

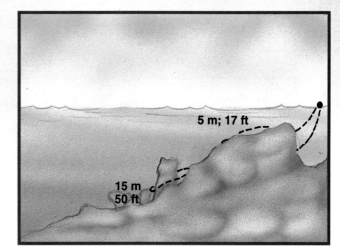

5 m; 17 ft

15 m
50 ft

● George Town

South Sound

N

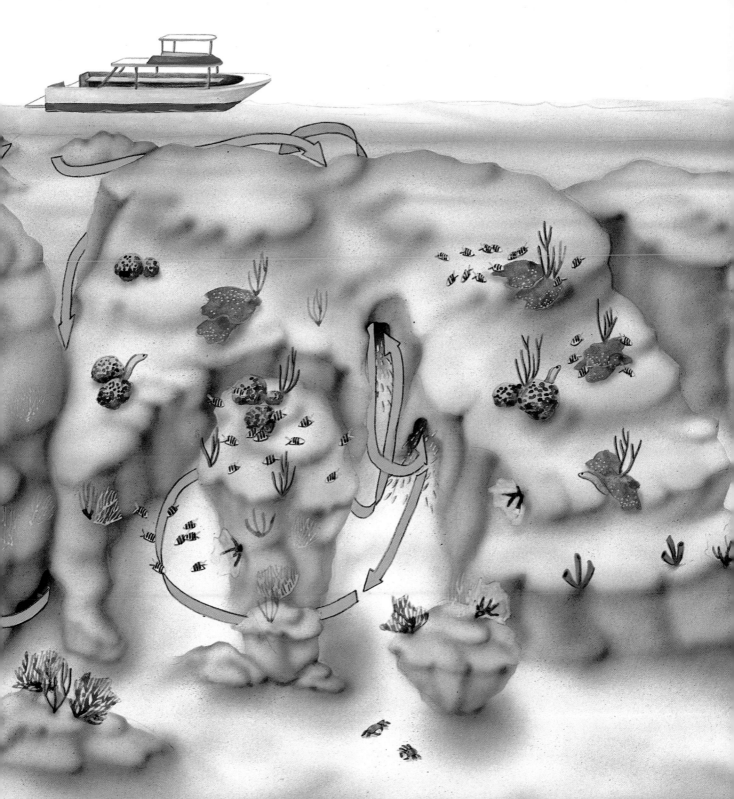

# Devil's Grotto

Bring a dive light to Devil's Grotto, even if you plan on making your dive at high noon. The caverns and tunnels aren't so long and enclosed, but a light will let you inspect many of the cracks and crevices that would be lost in deep shadow otherwise. Eels, lobster, crabs, shrimp, and a variety of bottom-dwelling fish can be found within the recesses of Devil's Grotto.

A

B

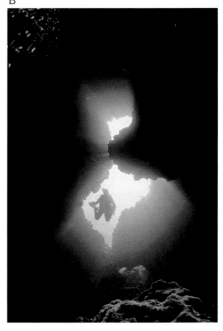

C

D

E

A. Devil's Grotto is a labyrinth of arches, caverns, and tunnels.

B. Although Devil's Grotto is riddled with caverns and tunnels, sunlight penetrates to most spaces.

C. Large silvery tarpon usually reside at Devil's Grotto.

D. A diver is framed by the opening of a deep cut in the fossilized coral that forms the maze of tunnels and caverns at Devil's Grotto.

E. Summer brings silversides by the thousands to Devil's Grotto.

This dive is a maze of swim-throughs, caverns, arches, and tunnels that cut back and forth through the foundation of the reef. The whole structure here is a gift from the past. It is the fossilized skeleton of a coral reef that started growing thousands of years ago, after the last ice age. Of course, there are still living coral colonies attached to the exterior of the mass, but the foundation itself is composed of calcium carbonate excretions built up over the centuries.

In late summer the tunnels are filled with thousands of shimmering silversides, which in turn bring in many tarpon to feed on them. As you swim through the passages, the silversides will open at your approach and close behind you, like a living cloud.

The schooling behavior of fish like silversides is thought to provide safety in several ways. Obviously, there are more eyes on the lookout, but the large number of fish may also distract preda-tors from effectively focusing on a single target. One of the amazing things about some schools, like the silversides, is that the individual fish do not just swim in formation; they also simultaneously feed on microscopic plankton in the water.

This is a shallow dive, but as with any other dive, it's a good idea to conduct the deepest part first, then work your way toward the surface. Keep a close eye on your depth changes while following the tunnels. When you've lost track of where you are in the three-dimensional puzzle at Devil's Grotto, you can easily find yourself inadvertently diving a sawtooth profile.

Devil's Grotto is located near shore between Eden Rock and Parrots Landing and is done both as a shore dive and a boat dive.

The water depth ranges from about 10 to 45 feet (3 to 13.5 meters).

Visibility normally varies between 30 and 60 feet (9 and 18 meters), depending on the tide and weather conditions. Currents are normally slight to none.

G

F

H

I

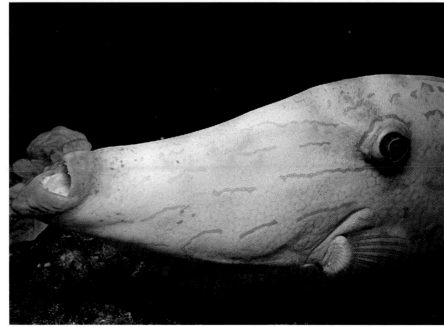

F. Caribbean reef squid, Sepioteuthis sepioidea, *school in the shallows over the reef structure at Devil's Grotto.*

G. The narrow reef openings at Devil's Grotto offer shelter to many fish like this honeycomb cowfish, Lactophrys polygonia.

H. Yellow goatfish, Mulloidichthys martinicus, *form protective schools in the shelter of the reef.*

I. During dives at Devil's Grotto one can observe scrawled filefish, Aluteres scriptus.

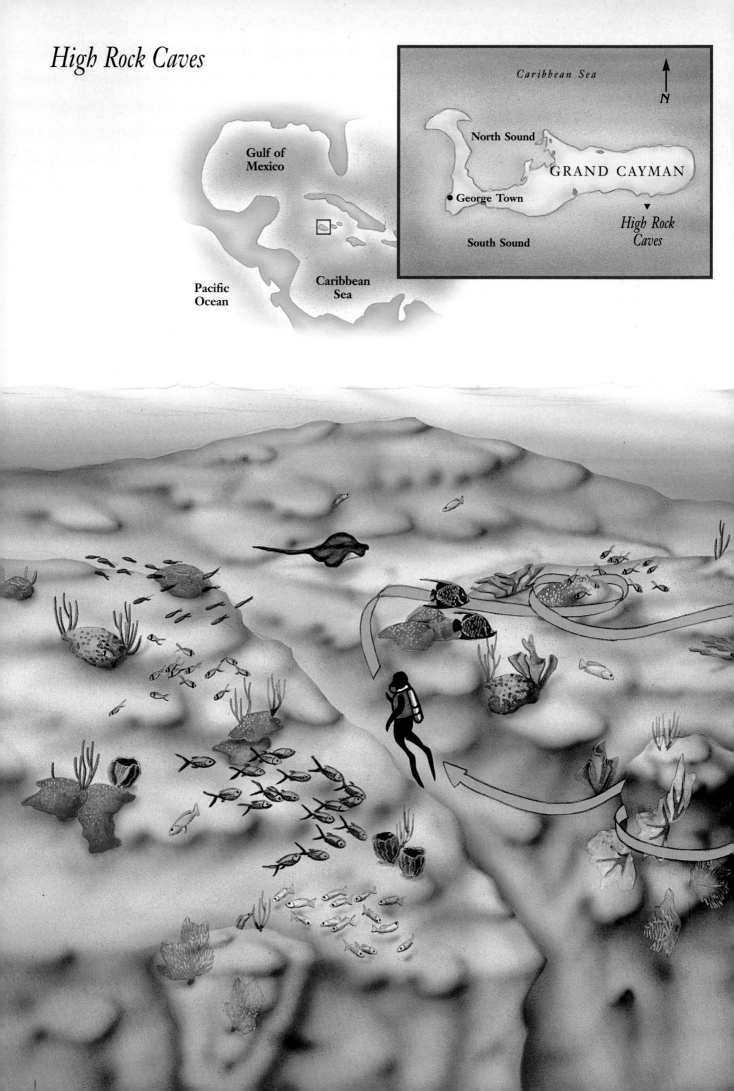

High Rock Caves

Gulf of
Mexico

Pacific
Ocean

Caribbean
Sea

Caribbean Sea

N

North Sound

GRAND CAYMAN

George Town

High Rock
Caves

South Sound

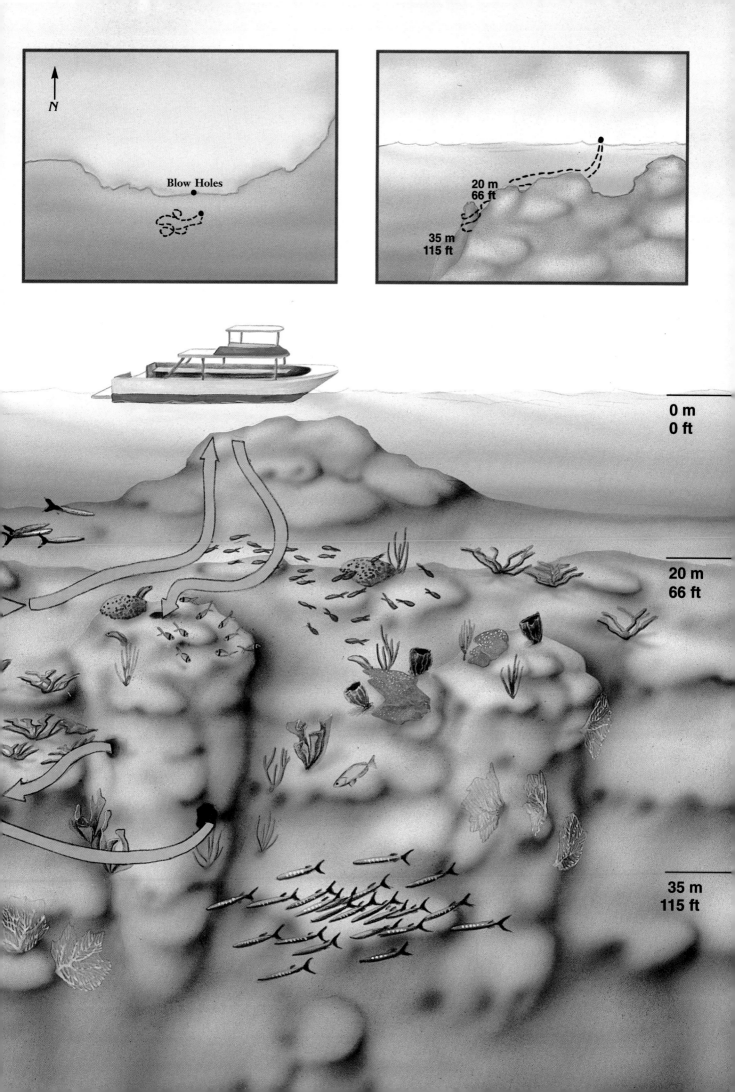

Blow Holes

20 m
66 ft

35 m
115 ft

0 m
0 ft

20 m
66 ft

35 m
115 ft

# High Rock Caves

The water above the wall is thick with Bermuda chub, Creole wrasse, bar jacks, and gray chromis. As you approach the top, look for a large brain coral boulder near the end of the most prominent finger. A narrow slot next to it marks a chimney. This is an exciting

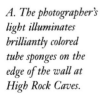
*A. The photographer's light illuminates brilliantly colored tube sponges on the edge of the wall at High Rock Caves.*

*B. Nutrient-rich waters allow many colorful life forms, like these sponges, to grow prosperously.*

dive in a vertical shaft that splits, exiting on either side. To the west it comes out at 85 feet (26 meters) amid a tangled profusion of finger and moose antler sponges. To the east it comes out around 105 feet (32 meters), surrounded by wire coral and finger sponges. Enter the chimney headfirst after you decide to exit on the deep side or the shallow side. Take care not to kick any of the marine life growing along the inside of the chimney on the way down. As you continue to the west along the wall, you will come to a

bulbous spur facing a pinnacle that nearly touches the wall. The seaward side of the pinnacle is nearly black with sea fans, while pale orange, yellow, and brown sponges cover the narrow slot between the pinnacle and the wall. Between the pinnacle and the spur there are two cave openings at around 100 feet (30 meters) in the face of the wall. The one on the right, as you face the wall, is a dead end. The left-hand entrance leads into a long tunnel that eventually exits on top of the wall at 65 feet (20 meters). The depth

*C, D. Two divers fly past the coral formations on high-tech Farallon diver propulsion vehicles. Thanks to the clear water at High Rock Caves, it is possible to make photographs with a complete view of the sandy bottom, of the reef wall, and of the colorful sponges.*

*E. A solitary great barracuda,* Sphyraena barracuda, *crosses the dark blue waters at High Rock Caves.*

*F. The vivid colors of a queen angelfish,* Holocanthus ciliaris, *are evident in this photograph.*

*G. This queen parrotfish,* Scarus vetula, *has apparently been photographed at night (notice the mucus around the fish which prevents nocturnal predators' assaults).*

*H. This peacock flounder,* Bothus lunatus, *has left its secure refuge at the sandy bottom and swims in the night at High Rock Caves.*

*I. The photographer's strobes illuminate a round coral formation in the dark waters of High Rock Caves.*

E

F

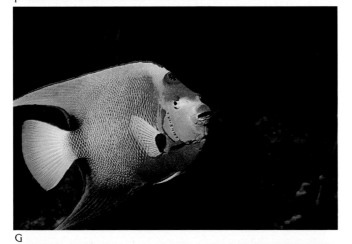

G

H

and confinement of the tunnel may make you hurry, but be careful not to exceed a safe ascent rate. Many crevices and small branches off the tunnel hide marine life.

There are also three sand pockets, each surrounded by a 10-foot (3-meter) high wall of coral. Stingrays frequently search the sand for prey, shadowed by a bar jack or coney hoping for a free meal. Groupers, moray eels, and lobsters inhabit the crevices of the mini-wall surrounding the sand pockets. Look closely if you see a moray eel or other fish beneath a ledge here, because a variety of cleaner shrimp live out of sight on the upper surface of many crevices. They

I

drop down only to pick the ectoparasites off host animals.

High Rock Caves takes its name from the High Rock community on Grand Cayman, located opposite the dive site. The top of the wall is about 65 feet (20 meters), and the three large sand patches are between 50 and 60 feet (15 and 18 meters). The coral ridges closest to shore rise up as close as 10 feet from the surface. Only a few dive operators visit this site on a regular basis due to its position, somewhat exposed to the prevailing winds, and its distance from most docks. Visibility is usually in the 70- to 100-foot (21- to 30-meter) range, unless the wind has been blowing from the east or southeast.

# Babylon

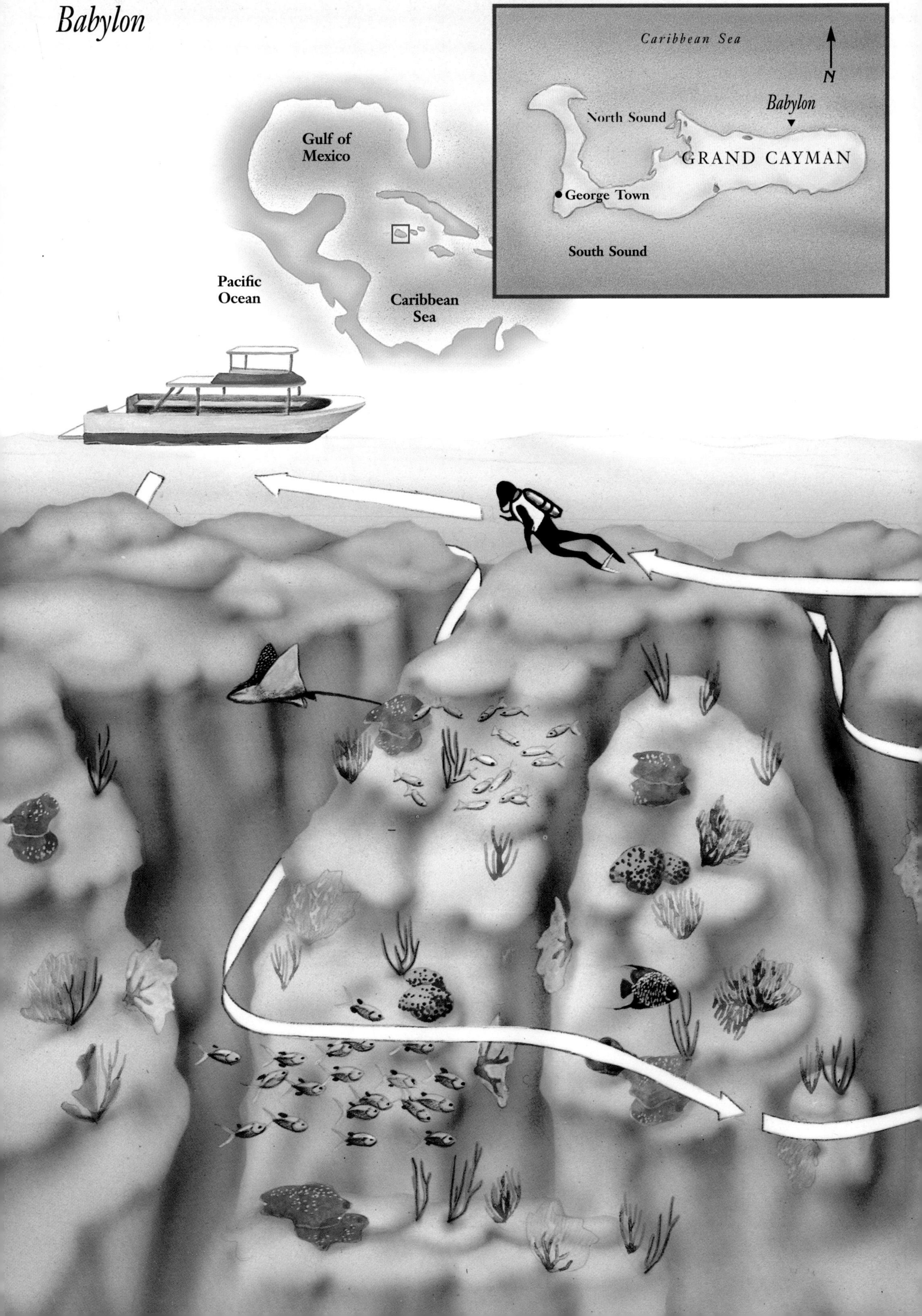

Caribbean Sea

N

Gulf of
Mexico

North Sound

Babylon

GRAND CAYMAN

George Town

Pacific
Ocean

Caribbean
Sea

South Sound

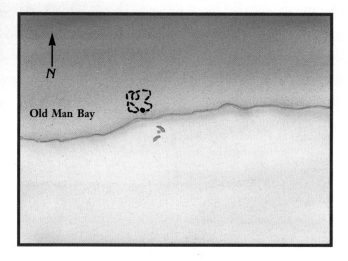

Old Man Bay

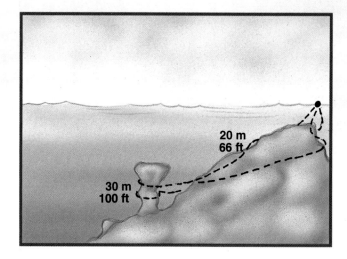

20 m
66 ft

30 m
100 ft

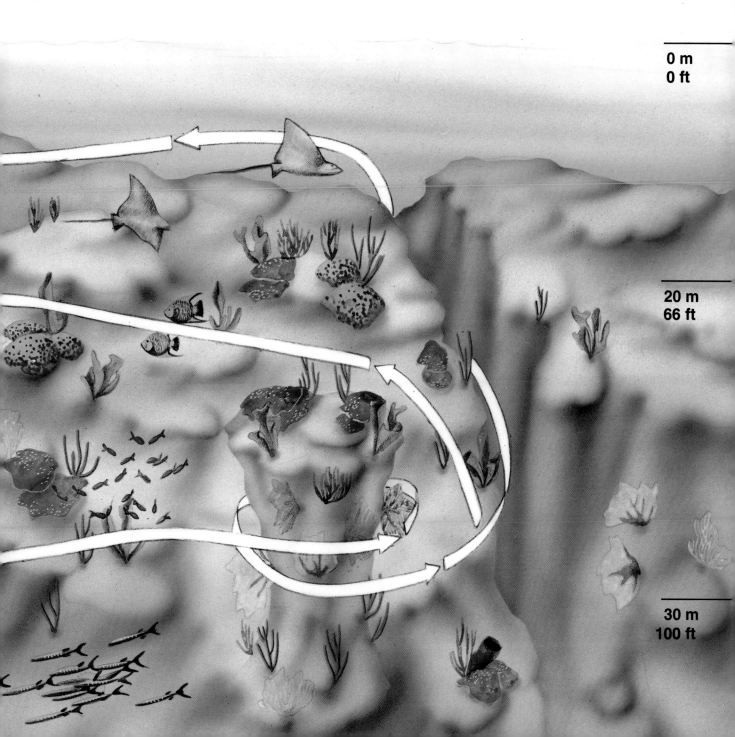

0 m
0 ft

20 m
66 ft

30 m
100 ft

# Babylon

The entire North Wall of Grand Cayman offers some level of quality diving, but diving is concentrated along the 45 or so "name" sites. Babylon is an example of one of the favorites. The dramatic seascape alone makes the dive worthwhile.

*A. A rare combination of azure vase sponges,* Callyspongia plicifera, *and strawberry vase sponges,* Mycale laxissima, *compete with a colony of giant star coral,* Montastrea cavernosa, *at Babylon.*

Located on the northeast end of the island, Babylon is often dived by live-aboard operations like the *Cayman Aggressor IV.* A handful of day dive boats also make the trip, generally those that depart from the nearby east end of the island or are fast and seaworthy enough to make the trip from some more distant dock.

The highlight of Babylon is an impressive pinnacle situated very close to the vertical wall face. A massive cleft in the pinnacle begins at about 90 feet (27 meters) and rises to about 60 feet (18 meters). Most of the vibrant filter feeders are found within this submarine crevice.

Large black coral trees and massive deep-water gorgonians protrude everywhere, while orange elephant-ear and tube sponges provide riotous color.

The temptation to swim through this highly decorated crevice will be high, but please resist. A careless fin kick or even exhaust bubbles, multiplied by the

*B. A diver examines a brilliant red strawberry vase sponge at Babylon.*

*C. A tangle of rope sponge deep along the wall at Babylon.*

D

within some recess along the wall. Control your breathing and wait. There is an excellent chance the eagle ray will swim close. And if this doesn't work, don't despair. There is still the face of the wall to explore, with its vertiginous dimension and vibrant hues.

Watch for the strawberry cup sponges found here as well. Normally about twice the size of a clenched fist, they look almost black. But when illuminated by the dive light or strobe, their magnificent crimson color is revealed.

*F. Babylon has many pelagic fish like this school of Atlantic spadefish,* Chaetodipterus faber.

*G. While diving, look at the blue open sea; sometimes you can observe an eagle ray,* Aetobatus narinari.

*H. This Nassau grouper,* Epinephelus striatus, *can often be observed at Babylon.*

E

G

F

H

*D. Looking closely at the coral formations, one can see very tiny life forms like this peppermint goby,* Coryphopterus lipernes, *on a brain coral.*

*E. A school of horse-eye jacks,* Caranx latus, *circle in the blue water over the wall at Babylon.*

thousands of divers who might visit this site each year, could eventually scour this site of its delicate beauty. Many other attractions can be found along the wall as well.

Savvy divers will keep an eye to seaward for possible eagle ray encounters. If one is spotted, do yourself and the rest of the divers a favor by not swimming after it. You won't outswim it, and will almost certainly hasten its departure.

Instead remain motionless, hopefully

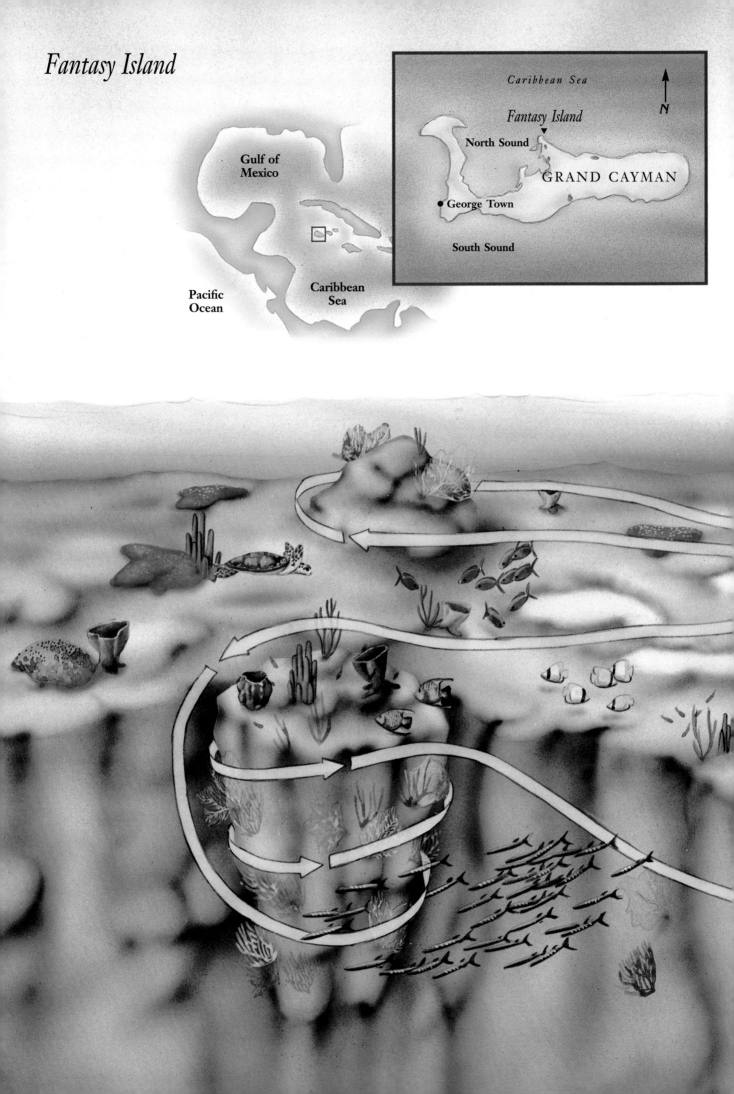

*Fantasy Island*

Gulf of
Mexico

Pacific
Ocean

Caribbean
Sea

*Caribbean Sea*

*Fantasy Island*

North Sound

GRAND CAYMAN

• George Town

South Sound

N

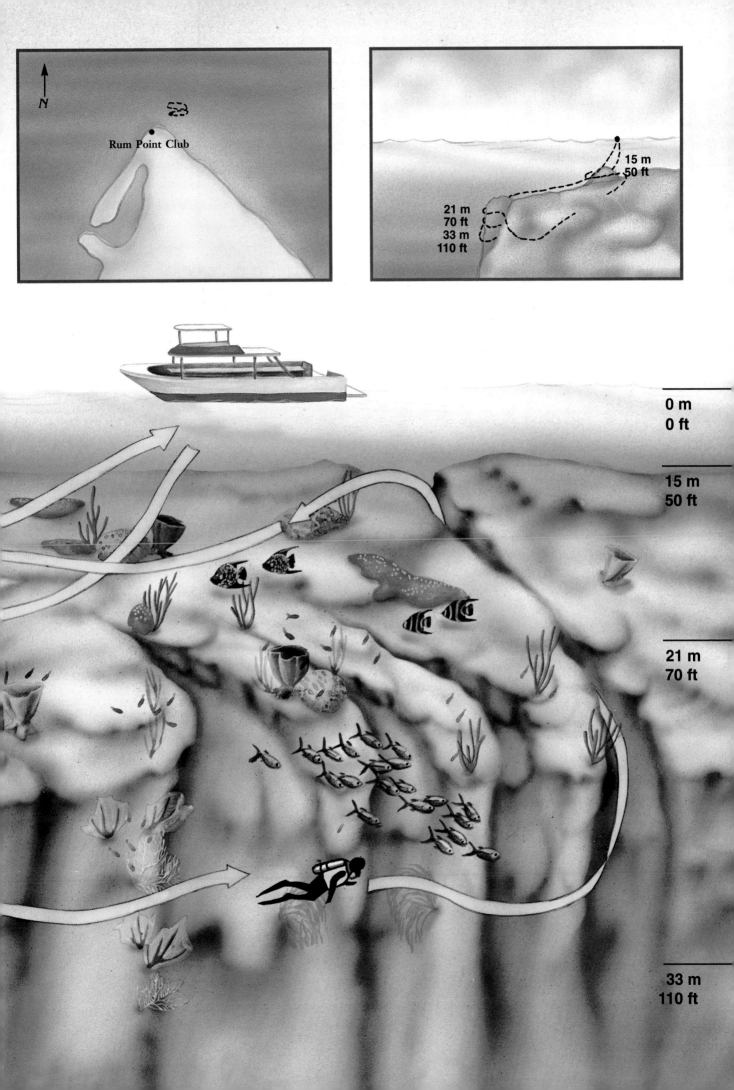

Rum Point Club

N

15 m
50 ft

21 m
70 ft
33 m
110 ft

0 m
0 ft

15 m
50 ft

21 m
70 ft

33 m
110 ft

# Fantasy Island

antasy Island is a particularly interesting section of Grand Cayman's North Wall, with a series of protruding spurs, a deep gully, and a pinnacle. The gully is on the west end of the dive site—the top is at 65 feet (20 meters). It begins as a very narrow slot, opening gradually into a vertical blue window. The pinnacle is at the opposite end of Fantasy Island. The top of it is also at 65 feet (20 meters), although the depth of the wall varies considerably between the pinnacle and the gully. At first you may not recognize the pinnacle. It is very close to the wall and looks like another spur from some angles. Up close you'll see that you can swim completely around it if you're careful. The pinnacle itself is one of the most overgrown parts of the wall. The sides are covered with sponges, plate coral, wire coral, and

*A. A diver pauses near a large colony of giant star coral,* Montastrea cavernosa, *at Fantasy Island.*

*B. A trumpetfish,* Aulostomus maculatus, *stays close to a vertical coral formation, trying to camouflage itself.*

A

C

deep-water gorgonians. On top the growth turns more to boulders of star and brain coral, interspersed with sea plumes and sea rods. Giant barrel sponges and green tube sponges fill in the spaces between the coral heads. If you see any of these sponges "smoking" during the late summer months, you've just witnessed a mass spawning event. The smoke is actually sperm, eggs, or fertilized eggs, depending on the species.

As you swim along the wall from the

*C. A diver approaches a cluster of sponges along the edge of the wall at Fantasy Island.*

*D. Hawksbill turtles can be observed at Fantasy Island. Here a diver swims with a beautiful specimen.*

*E. In the deep gullies or in the reef spurs live hidden many fish, like this coney,* Cephalopholis fulvus.

*F. A peacock flounder,* Bothus lunatus, *is hidden in the sand at Fantasy Island.*

*G. This red hind,* Epinephelus guttatus, *stops at a cleaning station on Fantasy Island.*

D

E

F

pinnacle to the gully, you'll pass a broad sloping section of the wall, followed by three distinct spurs. On top of the wall above the slope there is a large sand pocket that makes a good landmark during the dive. Usually the dive boat's anchor will be set in this pocket. The perimeter of the sand pocket is a ledge that harbors many small fish and invertebrates. A large coral-covered mound rises from the bottom on the side of the sand pocket away from the wall. Following the contour of the mound upward at the end of the dive will normally bring you near the dive boat.

Fantasy Island is on the North Wall of Grand Cayman, about a mile (1.6 kilo-

G

meters) east of the easternmost channel leading into North Sound. The sand pocket is about 70 feet (21 meters) deep, and the top of the pinnacle is around 65 feet (20 meters). The shallowest part of the dive is the sloping coral mound on the shoreward side of the sand pocket, at about 45 feet (13.5 meters). Like other North Wall sites, Fantasy Island may be too rough to dive when the wind comes from the north, causing the seas to build. Most of the time, however, the surface conditions are good. Visibility is usually about 100 feet (30 meters), with blue water. Because mooring buoys do not mark Fantasy Island, many dive operations choose to come here.

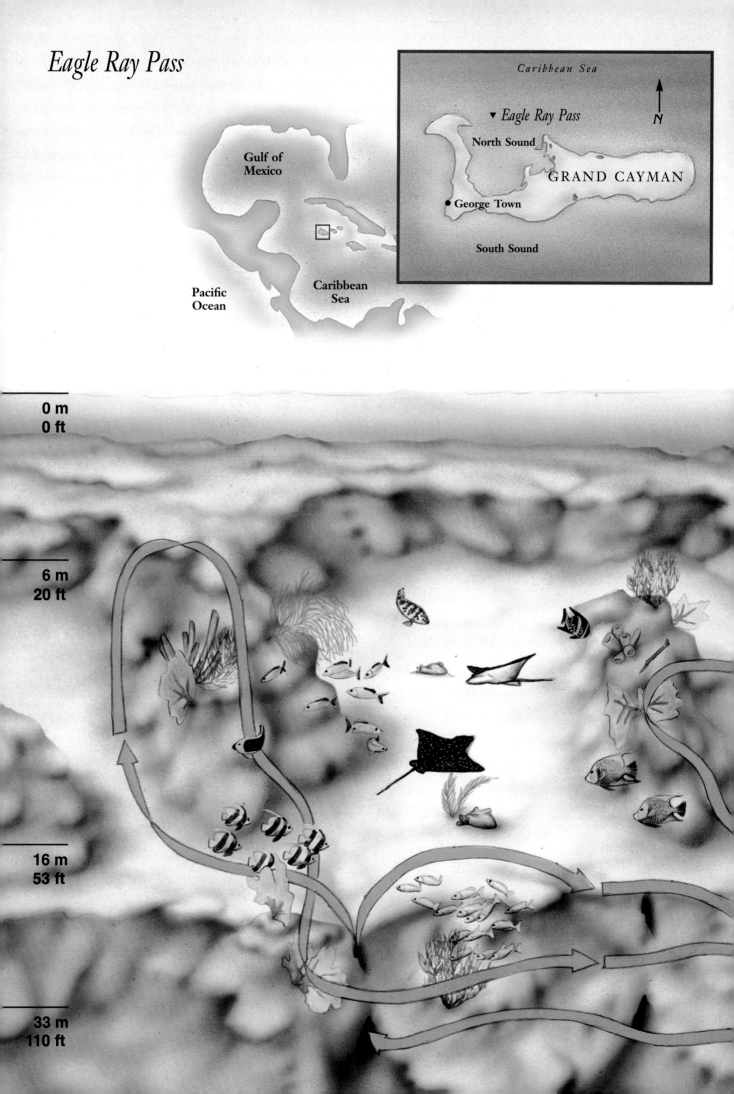

# Eagle Ray Pass

Gulf of Mexico

Pacific Ocean

Caribbean Sea

Caribbean Sea

▼ Eagle Ray Pass

North Sound

GRAND CAYMAN

George Town

South Sound

N

0 m
0 ft

6 m
20 ft

16 m
53 ft

33 m
110 ft

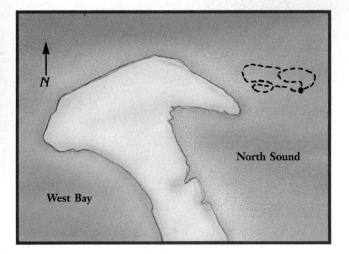

West Bay

North Sound

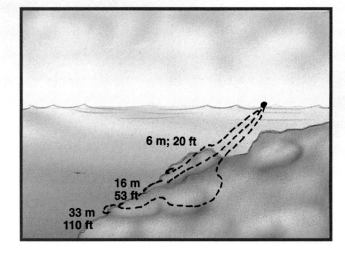

6 m; 20 ft

16 m
53 ft

33 m
110 ft

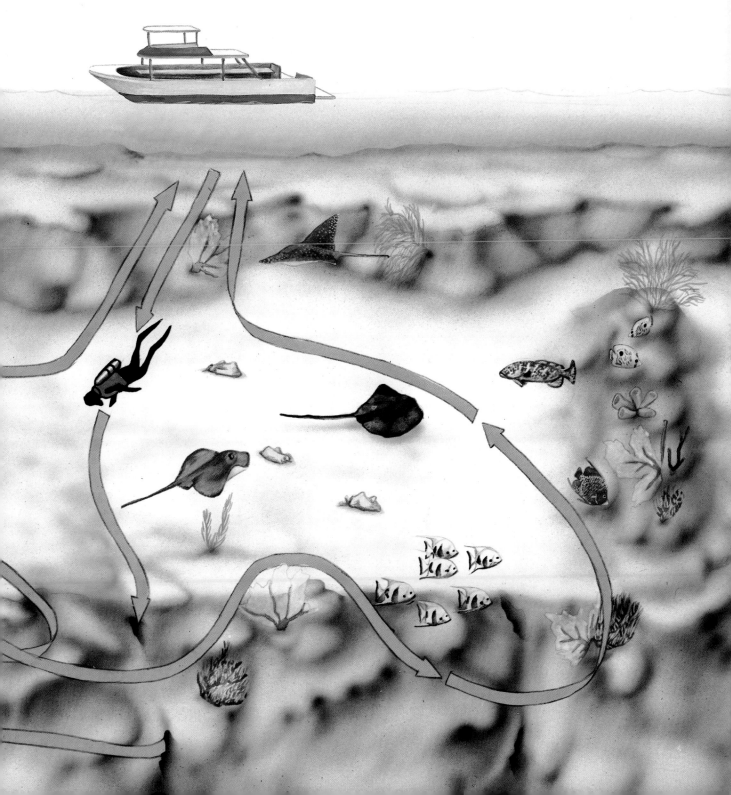

# Eagle Ray Pass

Eagle Ray Pass is one of those interesting places that makes you wish there were no limitations on depth or bottom time. Visibility is nearly always outstanding, and the topography is inviting. As you glide downward from the boat, details of the wall are already clear. You can see the muted green of mounds of star and brain coral along the edge and the brown of barrel sponges. Below you an opening in the

wall becomes a ravine that runs across its face like a staircase. At the base, a large coral arch frames the limitless blue on the deep side of the wall. A wide tongue of sand spills under the arch, making an easily recognizable landmark. To either side of the sand patch, coral promontories extend back up the wall, divided by smaller cuts. Whether you choose to turn left or right, you will find plenty of reef areas to explore.

There is no guarantee you will see eagle rays at Eagle Ray Pass, but it did get its name because divers see them here often. If you spend your time swimming along the wall with your

*A. Exceptionally clear water is the norm at Eagle Ray Pass. Here one can see a diver approaching the dive boat on the surface and a tubular sponge formation on the bottom.*

*B. A diver approaches a couple of French angelfish,* Pomacanthus paru, *near a coral outcrop at Eagle Ray Pass.*

*C. A squirrelfish,* Holocentrus adscensionis, *hovers nervously over a sponge at Eagle Ray Pass.*

*D. A diver admires a large cluster of yellow tube sponges,* Aplysina fistularis, *at Eagle Ray Pass.*

*E. A densely packed school of southern sennet,* Sphyraena picudilla, *illuminates the blue depths at Eagle Ray Pass.*

*F, G. Eagle ray,* Aetobatus narinari, *often seen cruising along the deep blue water off the wall and among the coral canyons that cut into the wall face at Eagle Ray Pass.*

back to the blue, you probably won't see one; they tend to swim parallel to the wall a small distance off or across the top of the wall a bit back from the edge. Early in the morning or late in the afternoon, you may be fortunate enough to witness an eagle ray feeding. Divers sometimes see them pushing their snouts into the sand, searching for molluscs and crustaceans. This happens most often in areas with a wide sandy channel with clear access to deep water. The rays will rarely allow divers to approach while they feed, but will tolerate being watched from a distance. After they leave, you can see the craters they leave in the sand, each about a foot

E

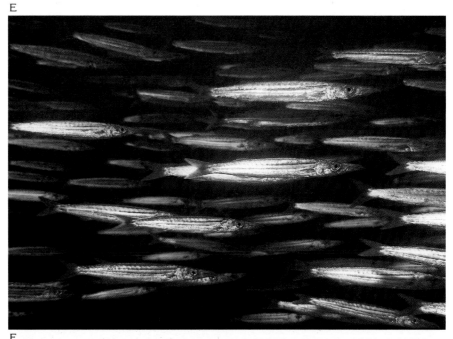

D

F

(30 centimeters) around and 6 inches (15 centimeters) deep. Eagle Ray Pass is adjacent to the central channel between the North Wall and North Sound. Depths range from 40 feet (12 meters) along the top of the wall to extreme depths off the wall. Visibility is normally in the 100- to 120-foot (30- to 36-meter) range.

G

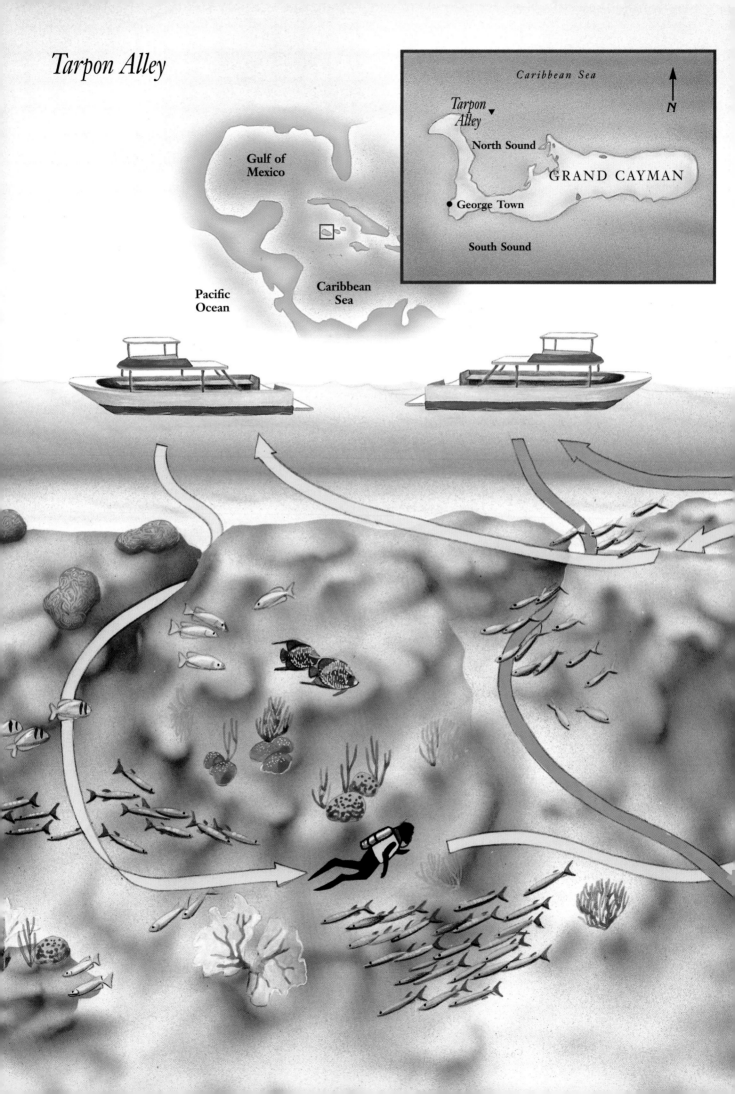

Tarpon Alley

Gulf of Mexico

Pacific Ocean

Caribbean Sea

Caribbean Sea

Tarpon Alley

North Sound

GRAND CAYMAN

George Town

South Sound

N

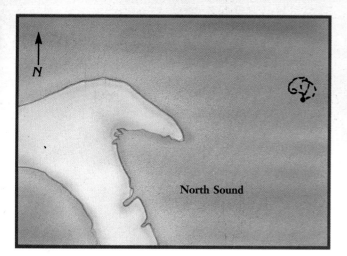

North Sound

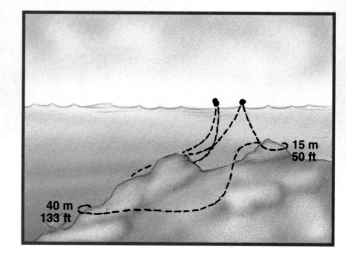

15 m
50 ft

40 m
133 ft

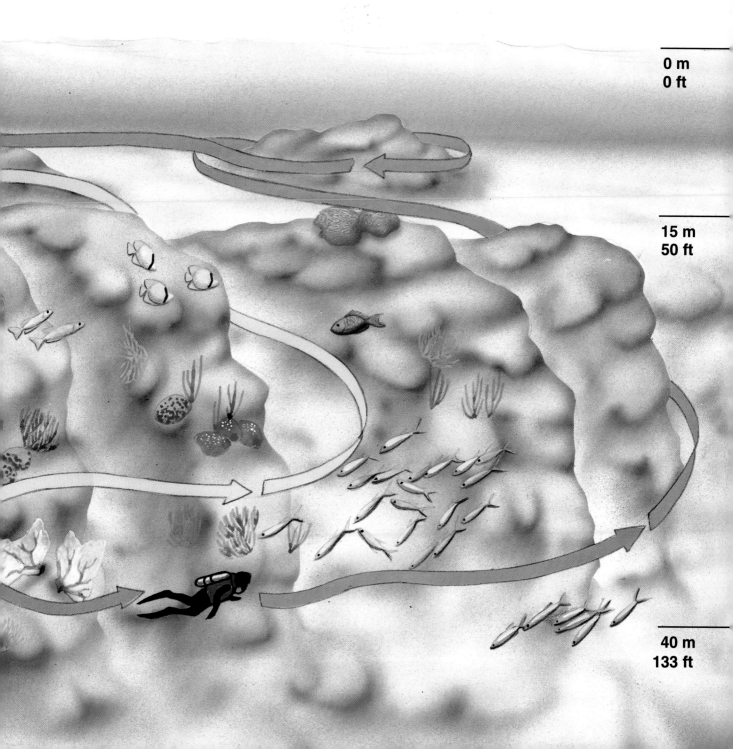

0 m
0 ft

15 m
50 ft

40 m
133 ft

# Tarpon Alley

You can actually expect to see tarpon at Tarpon Alley! The number varies considerably from day to day, but as many as 100 of them have been seen here at once. During the day they group together near the coral in the ravines or beneath over-hangs. With a patient, cautious approach you can get very close, unless another group of divers has already spooked them. Once they are driven

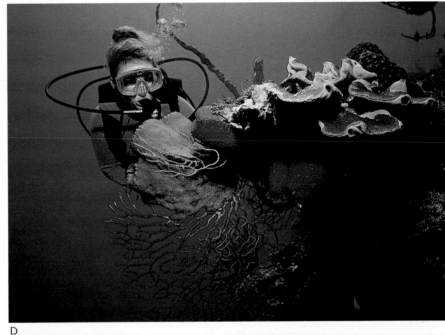

out of their favorite spots, the tarpon follow each other around the reef like a dotted silver line, eventually settling back in a protective cul-de-sac or over-hang.

Tarpon are voracious night preda-tors. They sometimes follow divers, zooming over their shoulders to swal-low fish illuminated by dive lights. Divers have also seen tarpon stalking fish schools in coordinated groups, but they are generally solitary hunters.

The name tarpon, taken from the Greek, means "large eye," a descriptive name that seems appropriate as soon as you see their large, black eyes circled by rings of silver. Although they attain

lengths of up to 7 feet (2 meters), most adult tarpon are 3 to 5 feet (1 to 1.5 meters) long and weigh 50 to 80 pounds (33 to 36 kilograms). Their brilliantly reflective silver scales make them notoriously difficult to photograph. The best bet is to compose your photo with the tarpon facing the lens at an angle, to prevent overexposure by your strobe.

The interesting underwater topography adds to the appeal of diving at Tarpon Alley. One large coral mound stands on the sand here, with three coral fingers wrapping partly around it and radiating outward. The resulting maze of coral ravines provides a lot of area to explore. Naturally, large numbers of reef fish are attracted to this rich habitat, including many angelfish and parrotfish, which actually eat the coral and sponges themselves.

Tarpon Alley is located on the western side of the main channel between the North Wall and North Sound.

Depths range from 50 feet (15 meters) on top of the wall to well in excess of 130 feet (39 meters) off the wall. Visibility is normally in the 100- to 120-foot (30- to 36-meter) range. Currents vary and can be strong at times.

E

F

G

*A. Tarpon,* Megalops atlanticus, *gather in groups within the protective culs-de-sac of Tarpon Alley.*

*B. Tarpon spend the day resting under the overhangs at Tarpon Alley.*

*C. A diver examines a brilliantly colored group of strawberry vase sponges on the edge of the wall at Tarpon Alley.*

*D. Gray angelfish,* Pomacanthus arcuatus, *can often be observed at Tarpon Alley.*

*E. A trumpetfish,* Aulostomus maculatus, *camouflages itself within the flowing arms of a sea plume.*

*F. Whitespotted filefish,* Cantherhines macroceros, *at Tarpon Alley. Whitespotted filefish can rapidly change colors, displaying or hiding their white spots and varying the shades of their orange bodies.*

*G. Sergeant majors,* Abudefduf saxatilis, *are plentiful in the shallower regions of Tarpon Alley.*

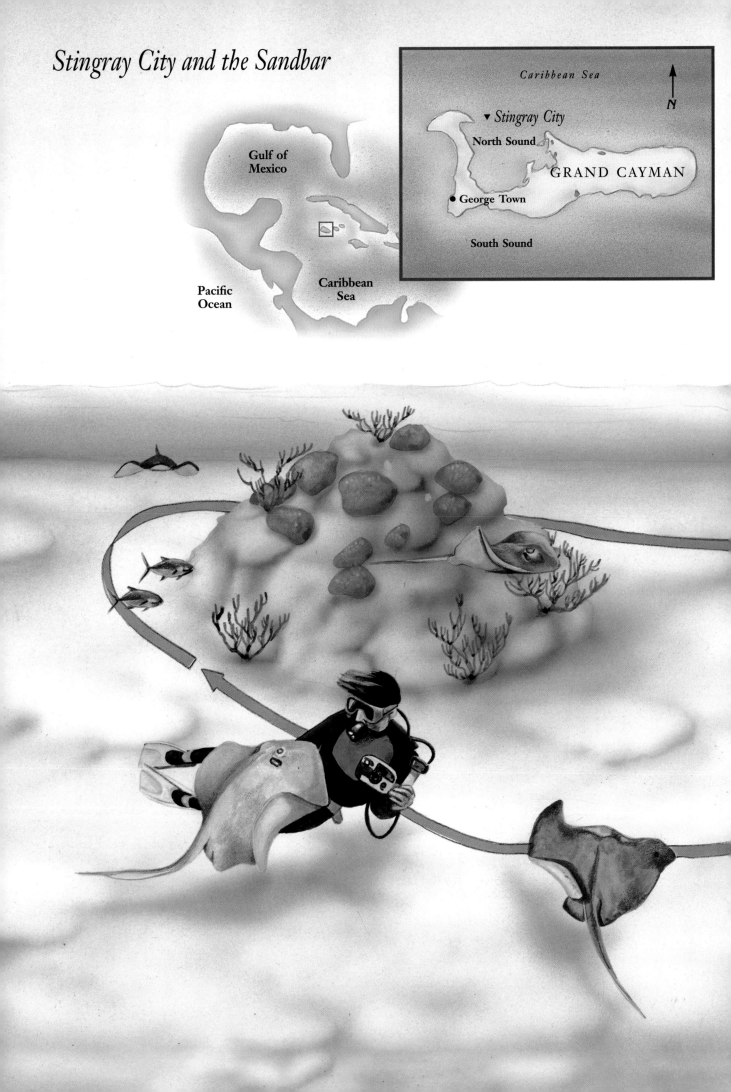

# Stingray City and the Sandbar

Caribbean Sea

**N**

▼ *Stingray City*

**North Sound**

**GRAND CAYMAN**

**George Town**

**South Sound**

**Gulf of Mexico**

**Pacific Ocean**

**Caribbean Sea**

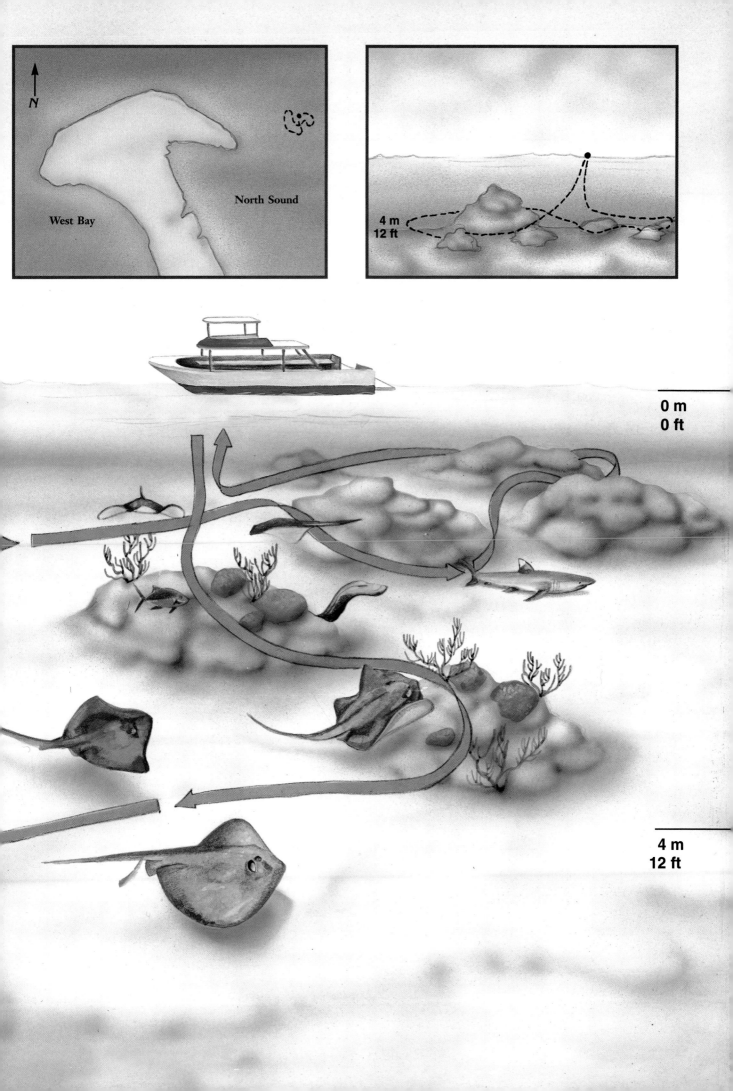

West Bay

North Sound

N

4 m
12 ft

0 m
0 ft

4 m
12 ft

# Stingray City and the Sandbar

A lmost every diver and snorkeler who visits Grand Cayman wants to add Stingray City to his or her logbook, and for good reason. This is the world's most famous 12-foot (4-meter) dive, for no other reason than the rowdy bunch of southern stingrays that flock to visiting divers for their daily handout of squid.

For many years snorkel and glass-bottomed boats operating charters out of

A

the North Sound would bring their customers to explore the nearby shallow reef. They would often anchor inside the barrier reef for their lunch break. The water was always calm here, and the turquoise color of the water made for an idyllic setting. The boaters would often toss scraps of conch and meat overboard. Over the years a group of southern stingrays, bottom feeders by nature, discovered this was a good place to score a free handout. By 1987 Stingray City had developed as a dive attraction as well. There are too many stingrays to count here, especially as they tend to band together in groups of 12 to 15 rays that

B

C

D

A. A diver feeding stingrays at the Sandbar; the photo clearly shows the shallow depth of the area.

B. A diver gets close to a gang of southern stingrays, Dasyatis americana, for a photo at Stingray City.

C. A southern stingray displays its underside, revealing details of its mouth and gills.

D. A southern stingray swims along the sandy bottom at Stingray City, probably searching for food.

roam from one feeding site to another. They range in size from babies barely a foot (30 centimeters) long to giants with wingspans of nearly 6 feet (1.8 meters). The original Stingray City location is still productive for ray encounters, as well as the conies, groupers, and eels that also dwell in and among the isolated coral heads that dot the bottom here.

The most famous alternate area is known as Sandbar, located some distance across the sound from Stingray City. Here a sandbar rises to within a few feet of the surface, perfect for those classic "over/under" shots of the stingrays flying over the sand. Another advantage to Sandbar, photographically, is that the sand is a bit coarser here and consequently falls out of suspension more quickly. Feeding stingrays is a sure way to generate particulate matter, and therefore backscatter becomes problematic in Stingray City shots.

Other sites have come to be known as Stingray Alley and Valley of the Rays. Be assured that no matter where you go,

if you have squid, the stingrays will follow. As the dive boat pulls up to the site, stingrays will already be grouped below. They associate the sound of a boat engine with food, but so long as there is no bait in the water, they will swim harmlessly, albeit inquisitively. However, once the bait container is opened, the tenor of the adventure changes. The rays are greedy and will swarm the feeder. Local divemasters are skilled in using bait to bring the action to their

F

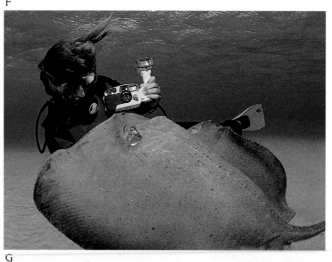

G

guests. They can prolong the activity by offering small reinforcement snacks to the rays, but even they must be careful: the rays might give them a little nip. Actually it is more of a suck, since their normal feeding pattern is to inhale their food from the bottom and crush their prey. They don't have teeth capable of producing puncture wounds, but bruises and hickeys are the proud badge of courage worn by divemasters pressed to Stingray City duty.

*E. A diver swims surrounded by some of the many fish that inhabit Stingray City.*

*F. This diver feeds a large ray at Stingray City to bring it in close for a photo.*

*G. This green moray eel,* Gymnothorax funebris, *seems to pose for a photo at Stingray City.*

E

# CAYMAN BRAC

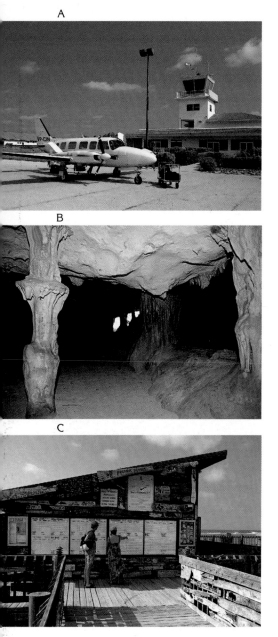

A

B

C

ayman Brac has some of the most gorgeous beaches in the Caymans and may be the most laid-back of the three islands. Yet it has a modern jet airport, good roads, and a fine hospital.

Situated 90 miles (145 kilometers) northeast of Grand Cayman, Cayman Brac is 12 miles (19 kilometers) long by just 1 mile (1.6 kilometers) wide. The west part of the island is quite flat, but to the east the island rises to a scenic limestone bluff punctuated with a number of small caves.

The resident population is about 2,200, and given the small number of resorts and condominiums available, even during the busiest tourist season there will probably be fewer than 3,000 people on the island.

Fortunately, the Brac continues to avoid the pitfalls of commercial development and has managed to retain its Old Caribbean charm. The Brac is safe, quiet, very friendly, and offers exceptional diving. The dive sites of Cayman Brac are lightly visited compared to those on Grand Cayman or Little Cayman, assuring that the mooring ball of choice will nearly always be available.

All of this, coupled with a resort infrastructure that includes only a pair of quality dive hotels and a handful of condos and guest houses, makes Cayman Brac one of the few minimally "discovered" world-class dive destinations in the Caribbean.

The entire southern shore of Cayman Brac consists of dramatic vertical walls, only some of which are marked by mooring buoys. Much of this area has no moorings and has been only minimally explored.

A. The interisland commuter at Gerrard Smith International Airport on Cayman Brac.

B. Peter's Cave, Cayman Brac, where local residents have taken refuge during hurricanes, including the devastating 1932 hurricane.

C. Divers check the boards for their boat assignment at Peter Hughes' Divi Tiara.

D. The emerald water creates a suggestive contrast with the white sand in front of Divi Tiara Beach Resort, Cayman Brac.

E. Divers explore the wreck of the Cayman Mariner, Cayman Brac.

F. Several large colonies of pillar coral, Dendrogyra cylindrus, can be found at End of Island. Unlike other hard corals, this species commonly feeds during the day with its polyps fully extended.

D

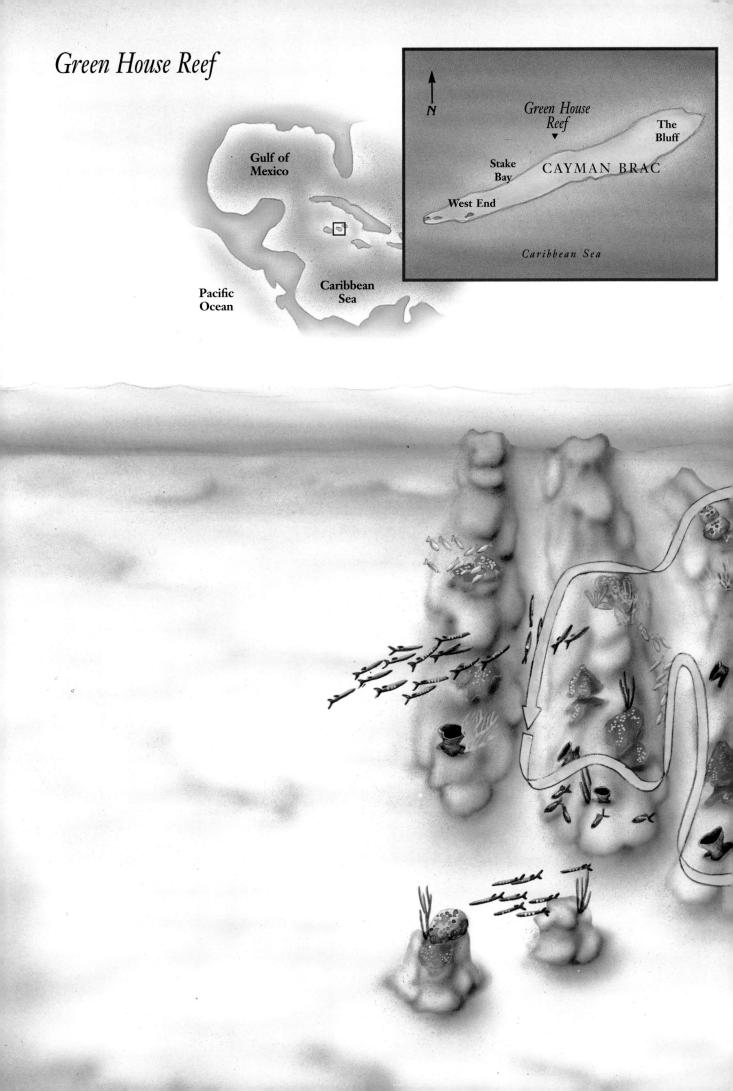

# Green House Reef

N

*Green House Reef*
▼

The Bluff

Stake Bay

CAYMAN BRAC

West End

*Caribbean Sea*

Gulf of Mexico

Pacific Ocean

Caribbean Sea

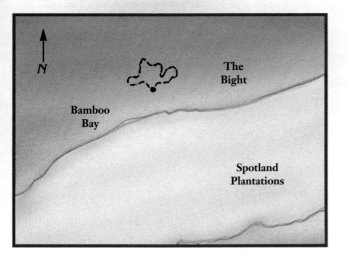

N

Bamboo
Bay

The
Bight

Spotland
Plantations

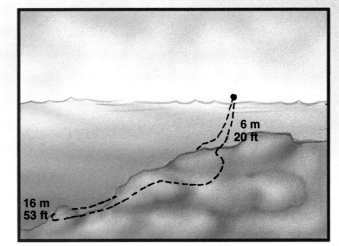

6 m
20 ft

16 m
53 ft

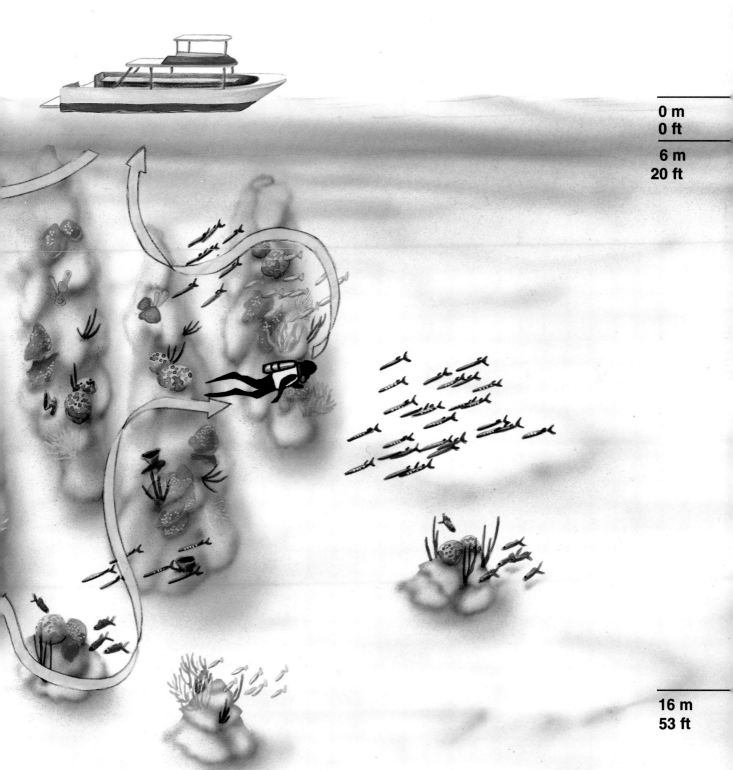

0 m
0 ft

6 m
20 ft

16 m
53 ft

# Green House Reef

Like many dive site names, the origin of this one is simple: there is a green house on the shore directly opposite the site. If someone paints the house another color, this dive site may have a different name!

The topography of the dive consists of the familiar parallel spurs of coral and sandy channels topped with many large coral formations. Some of the star coral heads are so old they have become mushroom-shaped, with a layered dome and a narrow base. Orange encrusting sponges mark the undersides of the

A

colony like age spots. These coral heads were alive when Blackbeard and his crew terrorized the Caribbean.

The channels between the coral spurs are deeply scoured at Green House, creating canyons with walls 15 to 20 feet (4.5 to 6 meters) high.

The living coral is primarily on top of the spurs, where sunlight is the strongest. The sides are covered with encrusting coral and sponges, especially leathery barrel sponges. The crevices along the canyon walls are favorite hangouts for schoolmasters and squirrelfish. Juvenile spotted drum can be seen beneath the smaller ledges. These

B

C

D

A. Large gorgonians capture a photographer's eye at Green House Reef. The polyps are extended on the fan on the left, and it is actively feeding. The polyps are retracted on the fan on the right, revealing more of the purple-colored flexible skeleton.

B. A school of grunts takes shelter among the corals of Green House Reef.

C. Nurse sharks, Ginglymostoma cirratum, can be observed in their shelters at Green House Reef.

D. A nurse shark swims over corals and sponges at the bottom of Green House Reef.

E. Large mounds of star coral, Montastrea annularis, are the principal reef builders at Green House Reef.

F. The sun's rays filter through the water's surface, showing the dive boat and the diver in silhouette. On the bottom the photographer's strobe illuminates a branching colony of elkhorn coral, Acropora palmata.

*G. A pair of banded butterfly fish, Chaetodon striatus, forage among the corals at Green House Reef.*

*H. Branching colonies of elkhorn coral grow primarily on top of the shallow ridges at Green House Reef.*

tiny black-and-white fish have a disproportionately large dorsal fin, which waves over the fish like a banner. As the drum matures, the fin gets smaller in proportion to the body of the fish, and it develops the spots for which it is named.

Barracuda are often seen patrolling restlessly from one end of the canyon to the other.

The tops of the shallow end of the spurs are about 20 feet (6 meters) deep, and the sand at the seaward end of the spurs is about 50 feet (15 meters) deep.

G

E

F

H

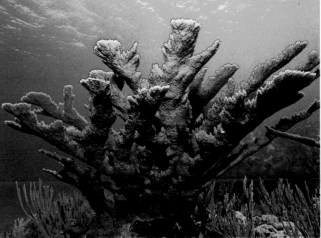

Coral mounds are scattered randomly across this sandy plain, each rising about 15 feet (4.5 meters) off the bottom. Green House is a great reef to just wander around, exploring whatever comes your way. The relatively shallow depth allows plenty of bottom time, and the parallel arrangement of the spurs makes it easy to stay oriented no matter how many turns you take. The visibility at Green House generally ranges from 60 to 100 feet (18 to 30 meters), with greenish water due to its proximity to shore.

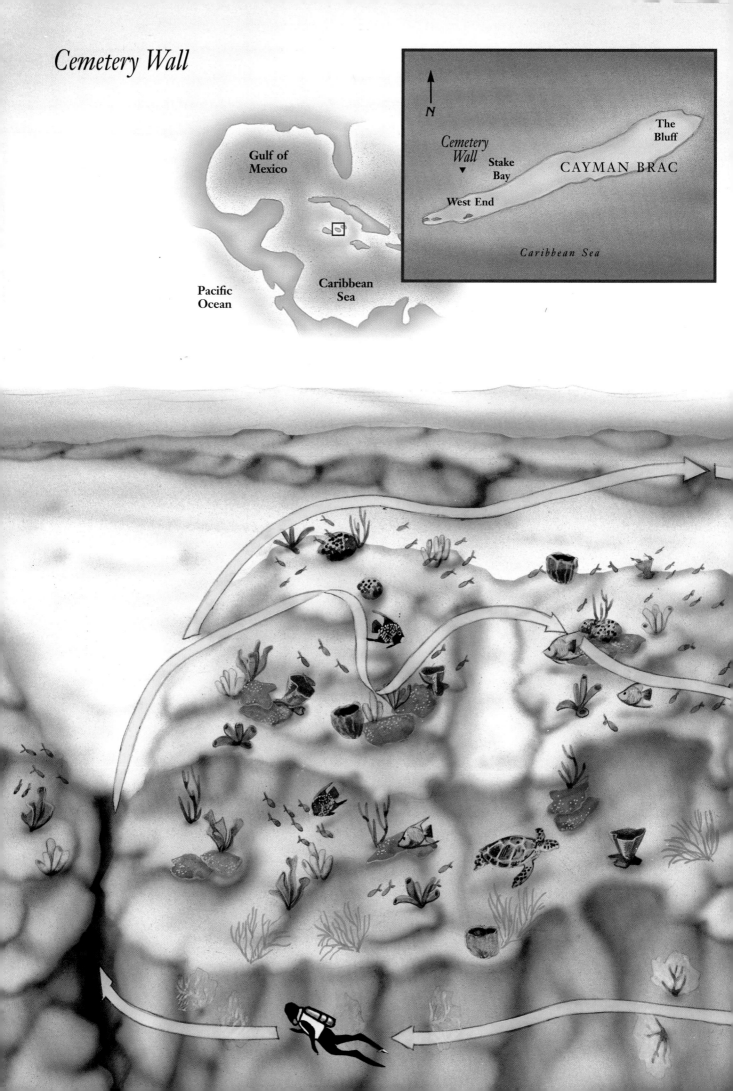

# Cemetery Wall

Gulf of Mexico

Pacific Ocean

Caribbean Sea

N

Cemetery Wall

Stake Bay

West End

The Bluff

CAYMAN BRAC

Caribbean Sea

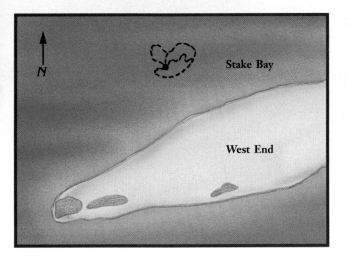

Stake Bay

West End

N

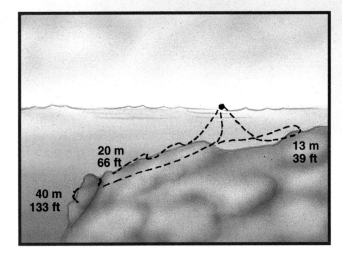

20 m
66 ft

13 m
39 ft

40 m
133 ft

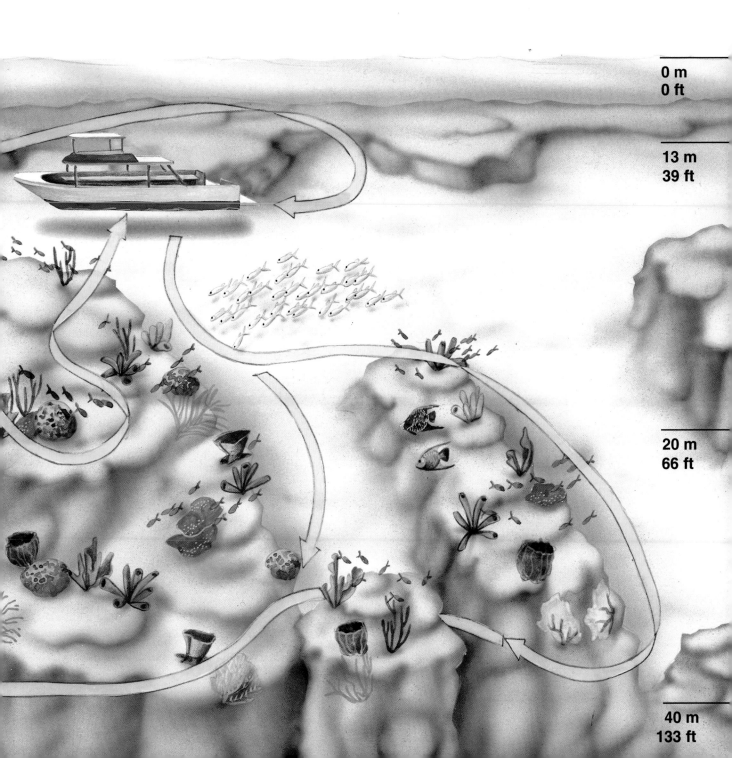

0 m
0 ft

13 m
39 ft

20 m
66 ft

40 m
133 ft

*A. A giant barrel sponge, Xestospongia muta, projects from the side of Cemetery Wall.*

*B. A diver approaches a huge gorgonian, Gorgonia ventalina, and a brilliant red finger sponge at Cemetery Wall.*

*C. Multibarreled tube sponges make a colorful foreground for underwater photographers on Cemetery Wall.*

*D. A large leathery barrel sponge, Geodia neptuni, competes for space with a colony of giant star coral, Montastrea cavernosa.*

*E. Caribbean reef octopus, Octopus briareus, can be observed at night on Cemetery Wall.*

*F. Brown tube sponges grow in profusion along the edge of Cemetery Wall.*

*G. Especially during night dives you can see redtail parrotfish, Sparisoma chrysopterum.*

*H. The photographer discovered a spotted scorpionfish, Scorpaena plumieri, well camouflaged by the coral formations at Cemetery Wall.*

A

B

# Cemetery Wall

A short tunnel cuts from the top of the wall to its face at the eastern end of this dive site, exiting about 20 feet (6 meters) down from the lip. From this point divers generally turn west and continue exploring the wall face, gradually working their way back to shallow water. The orange elephant ear, red finger, and green tube sponges on the wall are a substantial food source for the many queen and French angelfish seen here. The wall is also covered with hard coral colonies. Some are plate coral and some are star coral,

C

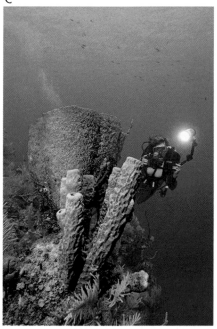

which normally grows in mounds or knobs. To tell the difference, look closely at the individual polyps. Plate coral polyps are elongated and form circles or spirals; star coral polyps are round and more randomly distributed on the surface of the colony.

Fast-swimming pelagic fish like blue runners and black jacks are often seen in the deep water along the face of the wall, but reef fish are more numerous on top of the wall. Large schools of yellow goatfish probe the sand, while the water column above the reef is filled with Creole wrasse, black durgon, and blue chromis. Several of the Caribbean

D

F

On the south side of the ridge, alternating sand channels and coral ridges extend toward the island. On the return to the mooring, you can wind back and forth across the coral spurs, gradually working your way to the boat. Soft corals and barrel sponges dominate the tops of the ridges, interspersed with more flattened hard corals.

Cemetery Wall is located on the north side of Cayman Brac and takes its name from the old cemetery visible onshore from the dive site. The top of the wall is about 65 feet (20 meters). Visibility is normally about 100 feet (30 meters), with blue water.

E

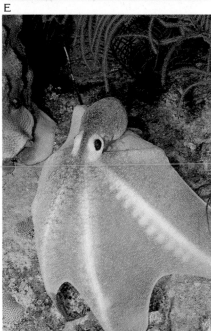

G

parrotfish species, such as stoplight and rainbow parrotfish, can be seen here.

The parrotfishes are responsible for a significant amount of erosion on reefs, turning coral into sand. They use their sharp, fused teeth, which resemble the beak of a parrot, to munch on coral, taking their nutrition from the algae and polyps, and excrete the calcium carbonate skeleton of the coral as sand.

Except for a few cactus corals on the sides of the coral spurs, the plate-shaped corals are replaced by mounds of star, giant star, starlet, and brain coral that form a continuous coral ridge along the top of the wall.

H

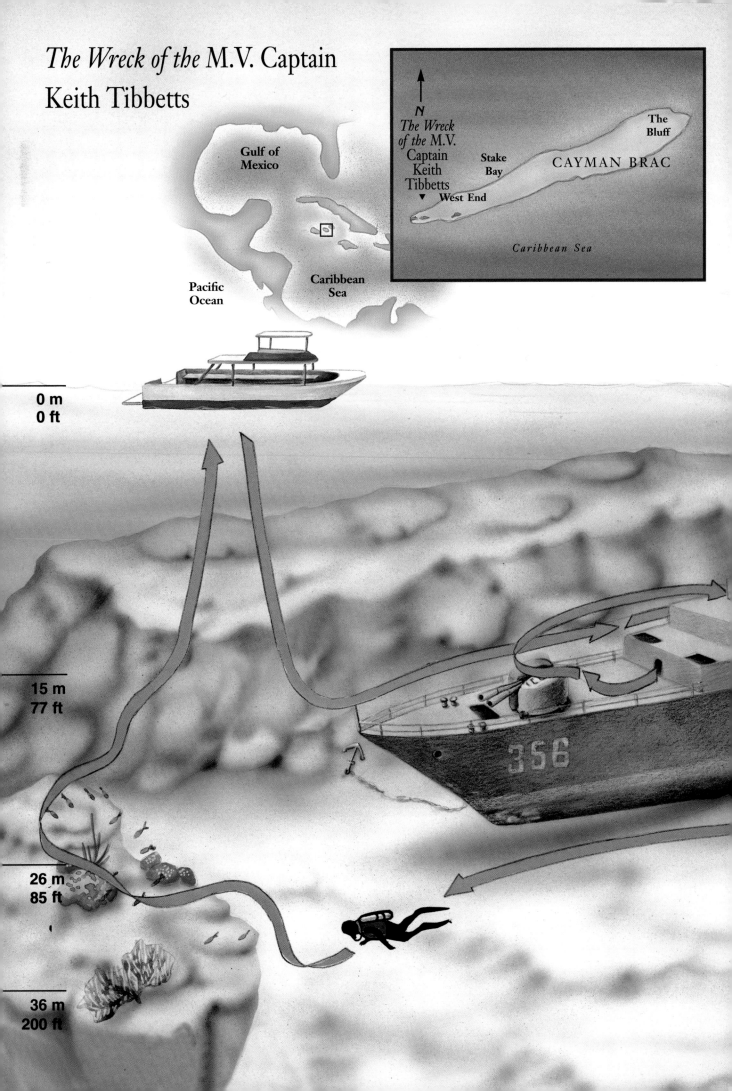

# The Wreck of the M.V. Captain Keith Tibbetts

**Gulf of Mexico**

**Pacific Ocean**

**Caribbean Sea**

*The Wreck of the M.V. Captain Keith Tibbetts*

▼ **West End**

**Stake Bay**

**CAYMAN BRAC**

**The Bluff**

*N*

*Caribbean Sea*

**0 m**
**0 ft**

**15 m**
**77 ft**

**26 m**
**85 ft**

**36 m**
**200 ft**

356

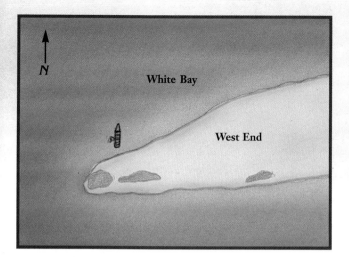

White Bay

West End

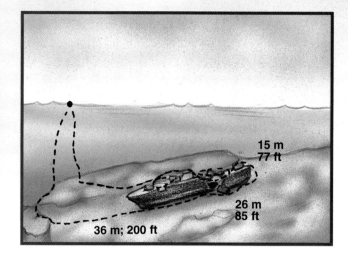

15 m
77 ft

26 m
85 ft

36 m; 200 ft

# The Wreck of the M.V. Captain Keith Tibbetts

A

Sunk as a dive site on September 17, 1996, the Russian destroyer *M.V. Captain Keith Tibbetts* is one of the most dramatically placed wrecks in the world. The vessel is perched on the edge of Cayman Brac's north wall, with the bow pointing out into the blue depths. Silhouetted against the bright morning sun, the tall, slender bow is an awe-inspiring sight. The twin barrels of the bow guns still extend parallel to the deck, reminders that this was once a proud warship. A similar gun mount is also intact on the aft deck. The ship was built in 1984 in Nakhodka, Russia, and carried the official designation number 356, which is still visible on the side of the hull. The ship is 330 feet (95 meters) in length and has a beam of 43 feet (13 meters). Her relatively light weight of 1,590 metric tons was achieved by using aluminum for the superstructure. Twin 10,000 horsepower turbines were capable of driving the ship at speeds in excess of 30 knots for high-speed pursuit. The ship was acquired from the government of Cuba and prepared for sinking by the

B

C

D

Cayman Islands Department of the Environment and local volunteers. She was renamed *M.V. Captain Keith Tibbetts* in honor of an influential local business-man, but dive operators may refer to the wreck alternatively as the "Keith Tibbetts," the "356," or simply "the Destroyer."

Two moorings are attached directly to the ship, one on the stern and one on the bow. Divers normally head directly for the bow, since this is the deepest part of the dive. The depth at the bow is about 80 feet (24 meters), with the sand falling away to about 110 feet (33 meters) directly under the tip of the bow. The forward section of the main deck is at 50

A. The slender bow
of the Captain
Tibbetts *slices
through the blue
water like a knife.*

B. The bow of the
destroyer is poised
dramatically over the
edge of the wall.

C. The Russian
destroyer's designation
number, 356, was
clearly visible in
several places on the
hull when the ship
was first sunk in
September 1996, but
some growth now
covers it.

G

Although the water clarity and relatively
shallow depth make the ship seem
immense at first, there is no need to rush
the dive. Most divers find there is ample
time to make at least one complete circuit
of the ship, pausing to enter the bridge
and several other interior areas. The guns
naturally draw a lot of interest, but the
most fish life can be found around the
intricate radar mount. Several schools of
mixed snapper hang around the mount,
using its metal frame for shelter. Only
about 20 feet (6 meters) below the surface is the shallowest part of the ship,
and as of this writing it is fully intact.
Visibility is normally 100 feet (30 meters)
or greater on the wreck.

E

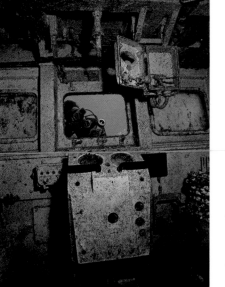

H

F

feet (15 meters), and the stern deck is at
45 feet (13.5 meters). The bottom under
the stern is gradually filling with sand,
but is generally around 60 feet (18 meters).
The ship is easily penetrated in a number
of places, in part due to deterioration of
the superstructure caused by storms and
seawater.

A large section of the center superstructure collapsed during a storm and
fell to port in the winter of 1997–98,
exposing entry points previously sealed
off. Take care when entering these newly
accessible areas, as there are many potential snags. Wreck diving experience and
equipment may be required to safely
penetrate some areas now accessible.

D. The twin barrels
of the forward gun
mount extend over
the clean deck space.

E. A diver peers into
the pilot house.

F. The propellers have
been working
themselves slowly into
the sand as the ship
settles.

G. The wreck seems
to overshadow
everything around it
for the first few dives,
but the surrounding
bottom is rich in
marine life like this
peacock flounder.

H. Portions of the
interior of the
Captian Tibbetts
have been opened up
for diver access.

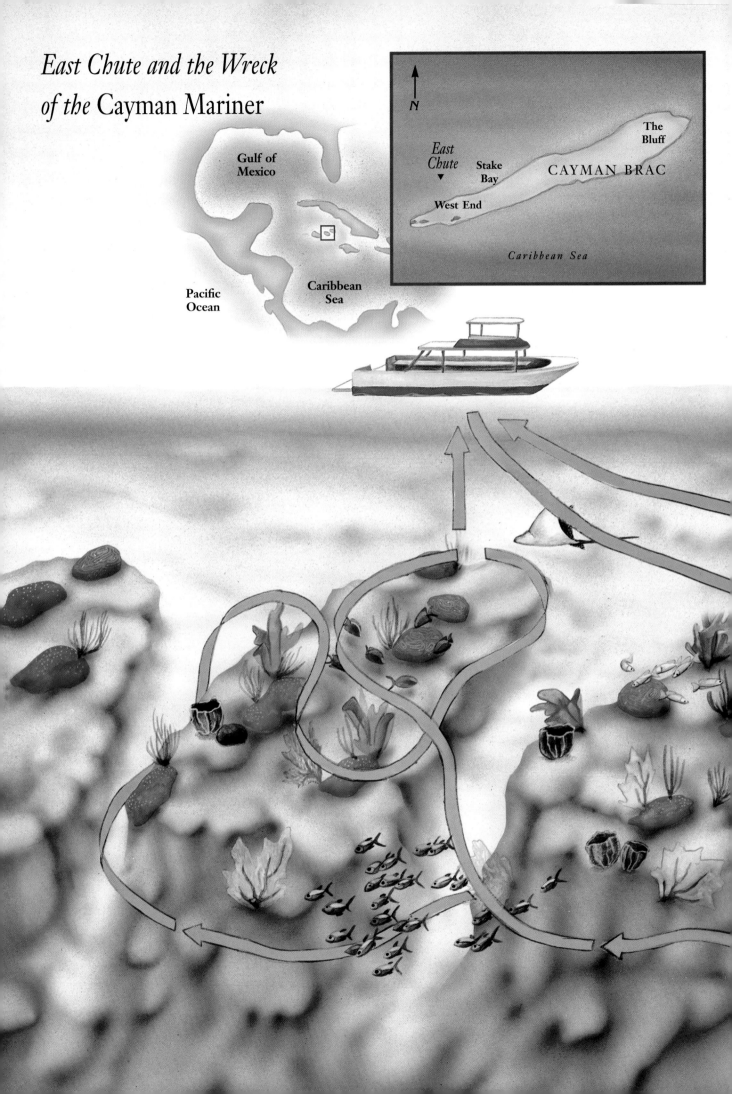

East Chute and the Wreck
of the Cayman Mariner

Gulf of
Mexico

Pacific
Ocean

Caribbean
Sea

N

East
Chute

Stake
Bay

The
Bluff

CAYMAN BRAC

West End

Caribbean Sea

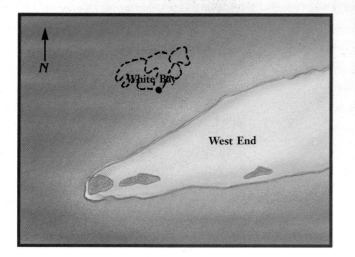

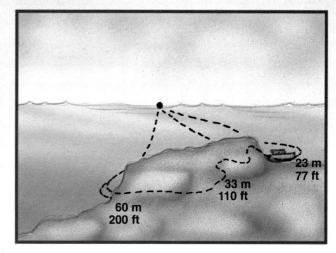

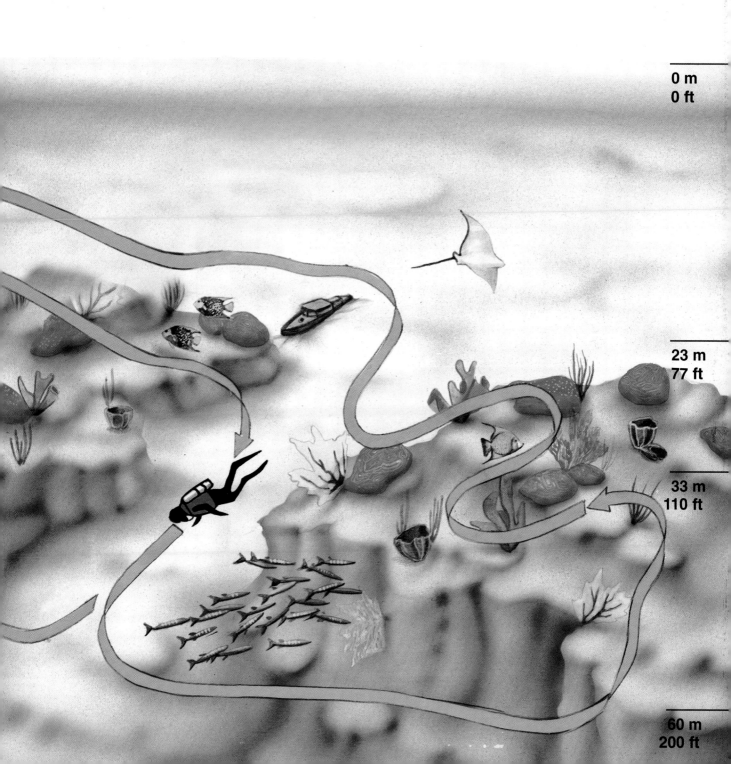

0 m
0 ft

23 m
77 ft

33 m
110 ft

60 m
200 ft

# East Chute and the Wreck of the Cayman Mariner

The word *chute* refers to a river of sand, which flows slowly, almost imperceptibly, from the flat area on top of the wall, through a gap in the reef, and finally falling particle by particle into the depths.

To a diver the chute merely looks like a deep sandy valley that divides the wall into two parts. East Chute is one of three

A

in the area; the other two are logically named West and Middle Chutes. On either side of the chute two large truncated coral mounds form the walls of the submarine canyon the chutes flow through. The mounds are primarily ancient calcified limestone, the legacy of thousands of years of coral growth. The surface of the mounds is still covered with live coral colonies, including many moderate-sized globes of brain and star coral. These hard corals alternate with gently swaying colonies of soft sea whips and sea plumes. The vertical face of the wall is lavishly coated with green tube sponges, orange elephant-ear sponges, and deep-water gorgonians.

B

C

D

A. The Cayman Mariner *is generally explored in the second half of the dive, since it is shallower than the outer wall.*

B. The upright hull of the Cayman Mariner *is well coated with encrusting corals and sponges.*

C. *A group of divers observes the wreck of the* Cayman Mariner *from above.*

D. *This diver swims alongside the wreck of the* Cayman Mariner. *The shape of this vessel can be observed very clearly because of the white bottom sand all around.*

E

Located on the north wall of Cayman Brac, East Chute is a relatively deep wall dive. The point where the sand chute breaks and begins to fall vertically is at 110 feet (33 meters). The gently sloping sand on top of the wall is about 70 feet (21 meters) deep, and the top of the coral mounds are between 45 and 55 feet (13.5 and 16.5 meters) deep. Visibility is usually about 100 feet (30 meters), with the brilliant cobalt water that characterizes the Brac's north wall. On the sand just past the shallow end of the coral mounds, you'll find the wreck of the *Cayman Mariner*. It began life as a Louisiana crew boat, designed to service oil rigs in the Gulf of Mexico. Willie

Ebanks, who still lives on Cayman Brac and is known simply as Grandpa Willie, eventually brought it to the Caymans. Grandpa Willie's old boat sits upright in the sand at about 55 feet (16.5 meters), covered nicely with sponges and encrusting corals. As you come up from the deep water off the wall, the *Cayman Mariner* is well situated for exploring during the shallow second half of your dive. The vessel is open for access from the top and is inhabited by a large variety of reef fish and invertebrates. Tiger groupers or crevalle jacks being attended by half a dozen cleaner gobies are frequently found at cleaning stations manned by neon gobies and juvenile

F

G

H

*E. A tiger grouper,* Mycteroperca tigris, *gets cleaned inside the wreck of the* Cayman Mariner.

*F. A diver pauses by one of the many colorful sponge growths on the wall at East Chute.*

*G. The cabin of the* Cayman Mariner *is open for diver access.*

*H. The coral ridges adjacent to the wreck of the* Cayman Mariner *are covered with large sponges and coral formations.*

Spanish hogfish within the hull.

A variety of anemones have tucked themselves into cracks on the bottom of the wreck. The giant Caribbean anemones have thick green tentacles, often topped with a circle of bright purple or pink. Corkscrew anemones are somewhat smaller and are easily recognized by their twisted tentacles. Pederson cleaner shrimp are nearly always present in the tentacles of corkscrew anemones, using their hosts as a base to clean other animals.

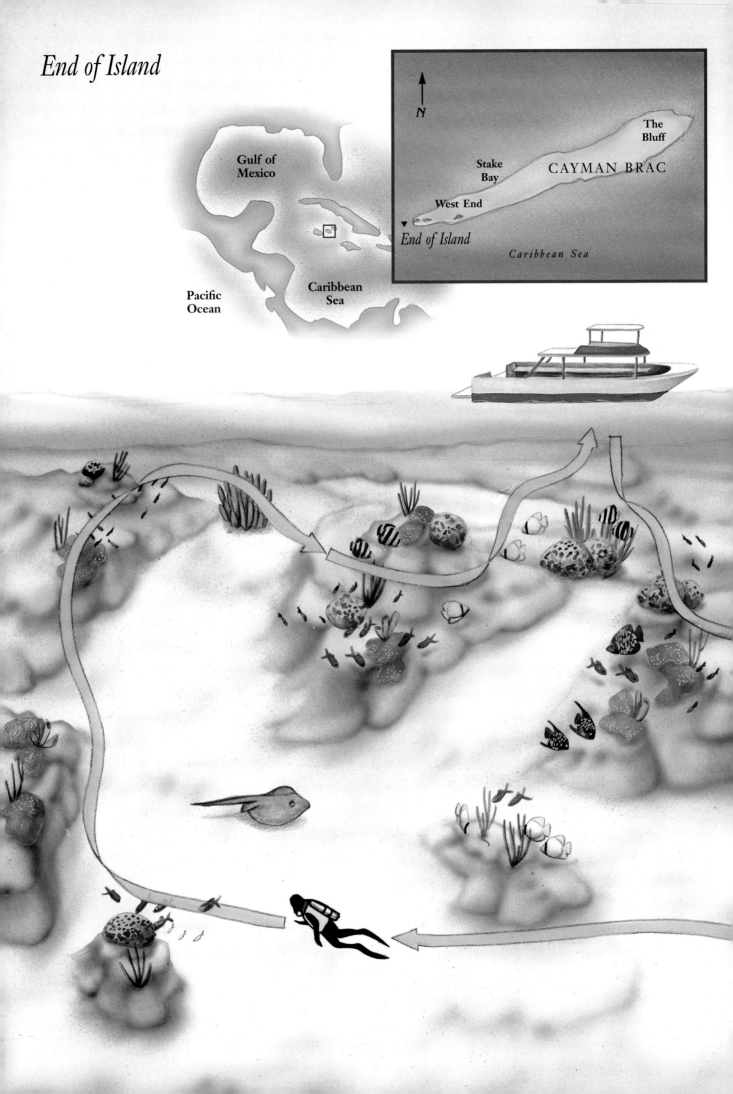

End of Island

Gulf of
Mexico

Pacific
Ocean

Caribbean
Sea

N

The
Bluff

Stake
Bay

CAYMAN BRAC

West End

End of Island

Caribbean Sea

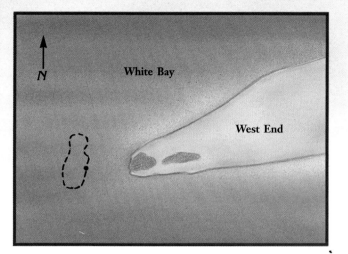

White Bay

West End

N

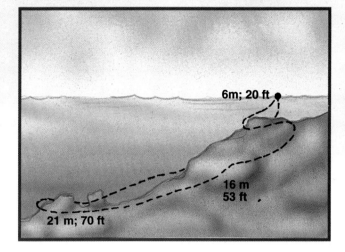

6m; 20 ft

16 m
53 ft

21 m; 70 ft

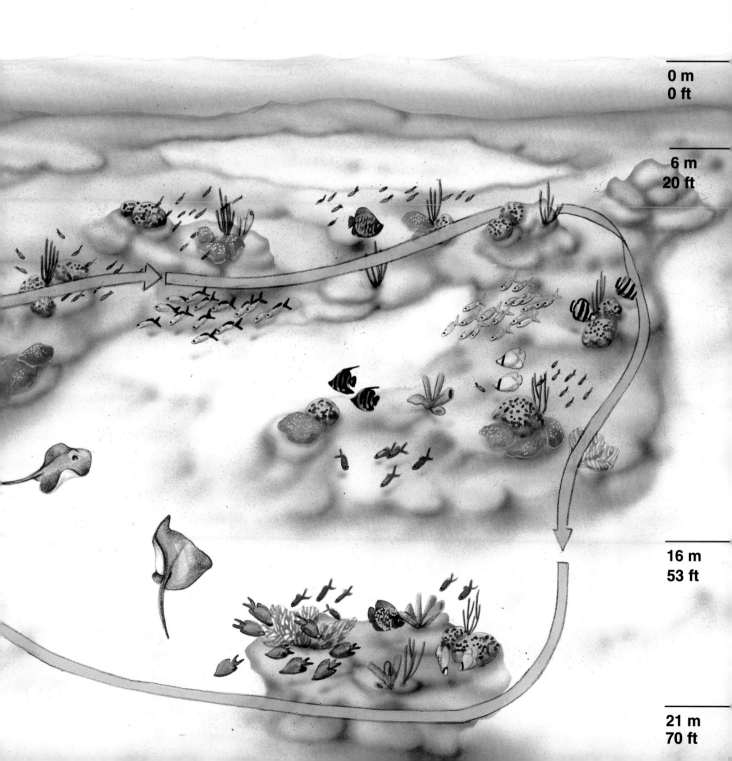

0 m
0 ft

6 m
20 ft

16 m
53 ft

21 m
70 ft

# End of Island

*A. Several large colonies of pillar coral,* Dendrogyra cylindrus, *can be found at End of Island. Unlike other hard corals, this species commonly feeds during the day.*

End of Island and Fishery are good for observing and photographing marine life. Both provide a sort of a mini-wall dropping from 20 to 35 feet (6 to 10.5 meters). There are high-profile coral ledges in the shallows that slope up to hardpan on the shoreward side, and to a sand plateau dotted with

A

B

C

D

coral islets seaward. Depths range from 15 feet to about 65 feet (4.5 to 19.5 meters), but a motivated swimmer could possibly make it all the way to the wall and deeper water. End of Island also features an intact pillar coral in just 25 feet (7.5 meters) of water. The pristine condition of this colony is amazing, especially when you consider the surge it has to contend with in the shallow water and the number of dives that are made here. But this coral remains

*B. Squirrelfish,* Holocentrus adscensionis, *can often be spotted close to pillar coral,* Dendrogyra cylindrus, *at End of Island.*

*C. There is rich marine life close to the huge coral formations at End of Island. Here a blue tang, Acanthurus coeruleus, swims close to a pillar coral, Dendrogyra cylindrus.*

*D. A banded butterflyfish, Chaetodon striatus, looks for food or shelter close to a pillar coral.*

*E. The spotfin butterflyfish, Chaetodon ocellatus, can be easily recognized because of its coloring.*

*F. This sand diver, Synodus intermedius, seems to pose for the photographer.*

*G. In the reef crevices one can observe many typical inhabitants of the reef, like this nurse shark, Ginglymostoma cirratum.*

*H. Diving at End of Island is quite relaxing. Moreover one can meet the most colorful life forms, like this queen angelfish, Holocanthus ciliaris.*

*I. A French angelfish, Pomacanthus paru, munches on a sponge.*

E

F

G

H

vibrant. With its polyps extended for daytime feeding, as is typical of pillar coral, it reaches to within 15 feet (4.5 meters) of the surface. It normally shelters a few tropicals like banded butterflyfish, coney, squirrelfish, or the exquisitely colored juvenile queen angelfish. Most of the schooling fish are found along the mini-wall or in nearby crevices. The sand flat is rich with queen conch and other sand dwellers like peacock flounder, razorfish, harlequin bass, and tilefish, while small oases of coral provide habitat for traditional reef dwellers like angelfish, trumpetfish, damselfish, and surgeonfish. The undercut ledges also offer refuge for nurse sharks. Even the hardpan environment

I

offers some fascinating marine life, including diamond blennies, smooth trunkfish, and yellow stingrays. Especially observant, and lucky, divers occasionally find flying gurnards here as well.

Although End of Island is an easy dive, currents can sometimes be significant. Visibility is usually 60 to 100 feet (18 to 30 meters), with slightly greenish water. When conditions are good, it is also an excellent night dive: the reds come alive in the beam of your dive light. A macro lens or close-up kit is excellent for getting great fish portraits and unusual invertebrate shots.

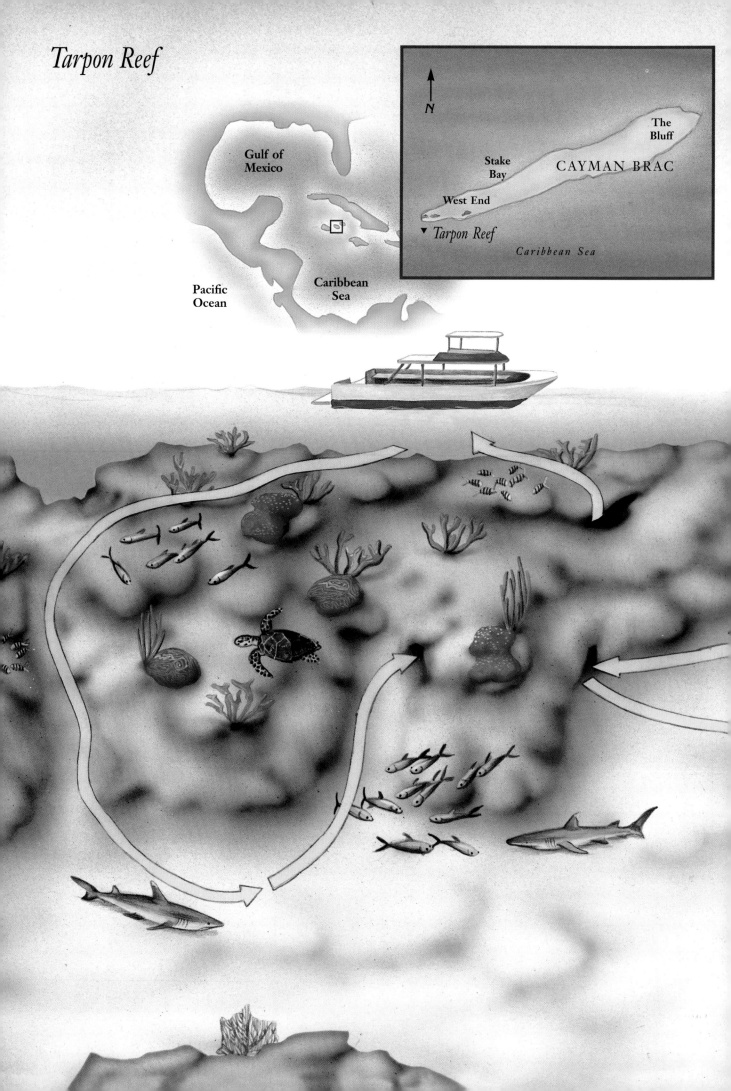

*Tarpon Reef*

Gulf of
Mexico

Pacific
Ocean

Caribbean
Sea

N

The
Bluff

Stake
Bay

CAYMAN BRAC

West End

▼ *Tarpon Reef*

*Caribbean Sea*

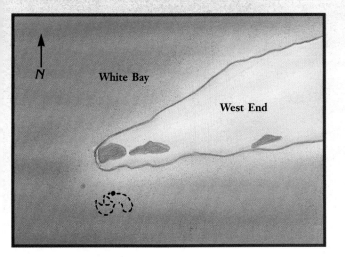

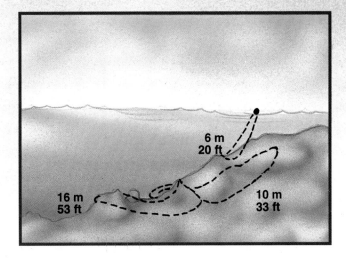

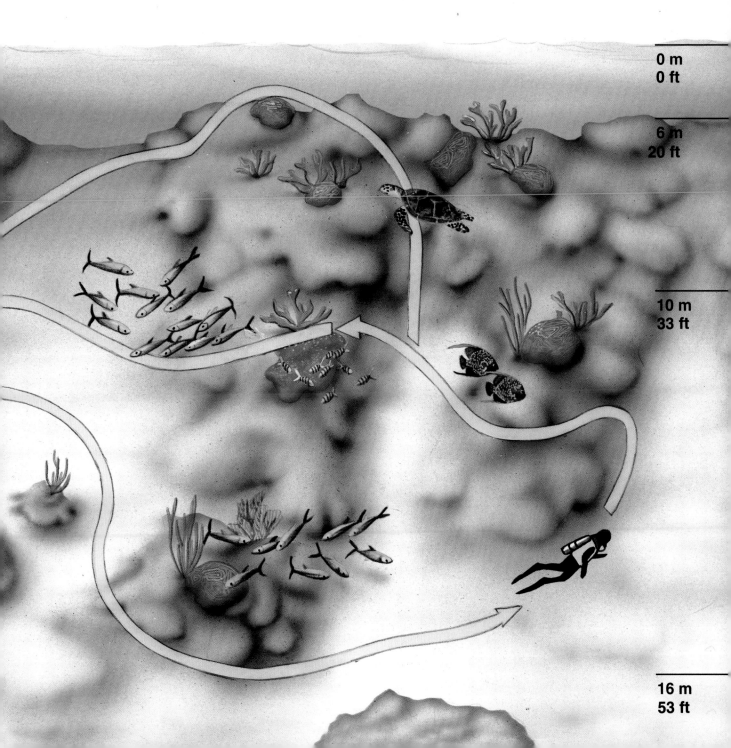

0 m
0 ft

6 m
20 ft

10 m
33 ft

16 m
53 ft

# Tarpon Reef

Tarpon Reef is a shallow reef along the south shore that provides a dramatic change from the deep, vertical profiles of the nearby wall.

The reef profile tops out at about 15 feet (4.5 meters), with the familiar spur-and-groove channels radiating to seaward, finally falling away to a sand flat in 50 to 60 feet (15 to 18 meters).

The corals are primarily boulder corals such as star and smooth brain, but there are a number of gorgeous elkhorn formations as well. This entire south

*A. A diver swims with a hawksbill turtle at Tarpon Reef.*

*B. A couple of tarpon,* Megalops atlanticus, *cruise the reef crest at Tarpon Reef, while the sunrays filter through the blue waters.*

*C. A tarpon, the fish for which this site is named. These silvery predators are normally skittish around divers, unless approached slowly and patiently.*

*D. A school of horse-eye jacks,* Caranx latus, *circles just above the coral at Tarpon Reef.*

*E. Scrawled filefish,* Aluterus scriptus, *can be observed at Tarpon Reef.*

*F. Macrophotography shows divers a queen conch,* Strombus gigas, *in the sand at Tarpon Reef.*

shore was once massively decorated with elkhorn until Hurricane Gilbert scoured the shallows. The south side of Grand Cayman was likewise affected, but both areas have come back nicely in the past decade. Fortunately, branching corals grow relatively quickly, especially in the clear water and strong sun of the Caymans.

As the name suggests, the highlight of Tarpon Reef is a resident group of tarpon. Unlike the tarpon at Grand

G

E

F

H

Cayman's Tarpon Alley or Bonnie's Arch, these tarpon hang together in smaller groups of 6 to 10 and are quite skittish. Perhaps they are so infrequently visited they have not become accustomed to exhaust bubbles, or perhaps the terrain makes it easier for them to disperse rather than hide. Whatever the reason, divers rarely are able to get closer than 6 feet (1.8 meters) here. If you get closer, congratulate yourself on a slow, controlled, nonthreatening approach.

Of course there is other marine life at this site as well, particularly small hawksbill turtles, bermuda chub, schools of colorfully striped sergeant major, French angelfish, and Spanish lobster. Given the predilection of hawksbill turtles for sponges, it shouldn't be too surprising to see them frequently at Tarpon Reef, since there is a large number of sponge species here.

Dive operators report that for some reason in the past year or so sightings of nurse sharks seem to be more frequent.

*G. A coney,* Cephalopholis fulvus, *in the golden phase at night on Tarpon Reef.*

*H. This close-up shows the eye and gill opening of a southern stingray,* Dasyatis americana, *buried in the sand at Tarpon Reef.*

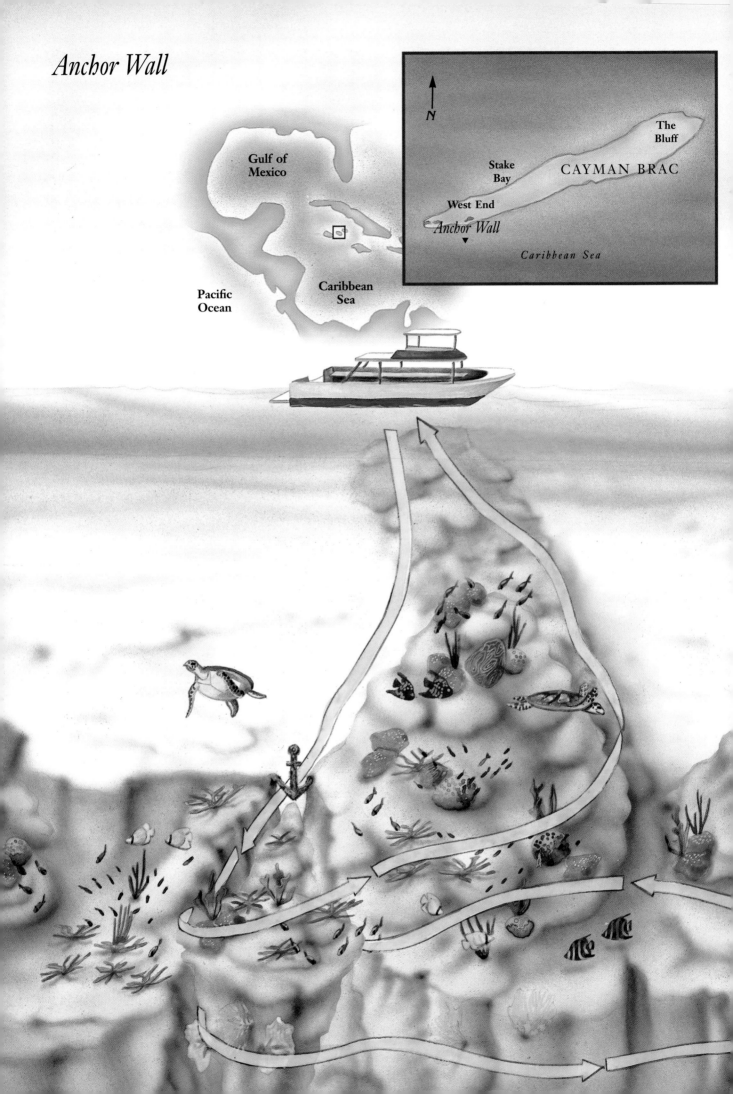

Anchor Wall

Gulf of
Mexico

Pacific
Ocean

Caribbean
Sea

The
Bluff

Stake
Bay

CAYMAN BRAC

West End

*Anchor Wall*

▼

*Caribbean Sea*

N

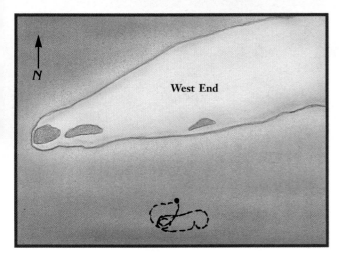

West End

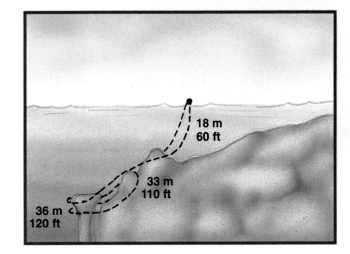

18 m
60 ft

33 m
110 ft

36 m
120 ft

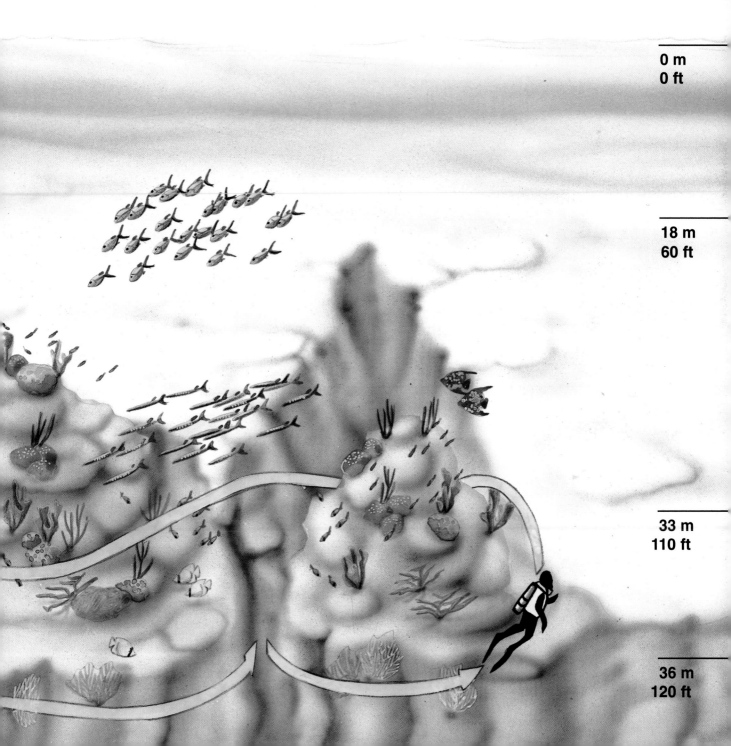

0 m
0 ft

18 m
60 ft

33 m
110 ft

36 m
120 ft

# Anchor Wall

Time has obscured the origin of the anchor that gives this site its name. Presumably some island freighter was anchored along the south shore when wind or seas caused its anchor to drag. Because there is no wreckage nearby, not even a chain attached to the anchor, it seems likely that no marine disaster ensued, and the chain was probably later salvaged. When you see how securely the anchor is stuck in the coral canyon, you'll understand why it was never recovered. The anchor itself is about 7 feet (2.1 meters) tall and approximately 6 feet (1.8 meters) across at the flukes.

The sand bottom in the crevice is about 100 feet (30 meters), and the anchor rests about 4 feet (1.2 meters) from the bottom, allowing just enough room for a diver to swim beneath. One fluke is buried in the coral, but the

B

C

*A. A diver watches a trumpetfish camouflaging itself within the branches of a sea plume on top of Anchor Wall.*

*B. Convoluted barrel sponges,* Aplysina lacunosa, *proliferate at Anchor Wall.*

A

second fluke remains exposed.

Sponge and coral now cloak the anchor, making it a fascinating wide-angle foreground for diver portraits. Care should be exercised to avoid stirring up the sand bottom or allowing bubbles to dislodge debris from above, or your photo opportunity may be cut short.

Passing through any of the crevices near the anchor will provide a convoluted pathway to a vertical wall.

The top of the buttresses is around

*C. This anchor, wedged irretrievably in the coral, gives Anchor Wall its name.*

*D. A tiger grouper,* Mycteroperca tigris, *waits patiently as cleaner gobies do their jobs.*

*E. A spotfin butterflyfish, Chaetodon ocellatus, shows its night colors on Anchor Wall.*

*F. An orange filefish, Aluterus schoepfi, is probably looking for nourishment close to coral formations at Anchor Wall.*

65 feet (19.5 meters) deep, but the surge channels are deeper and exit the wall at 80 to 100 feet (24 to 30 meters). Whether you head left or right from the anchor, the growth on the wall is similar—large antler sponge, orange elephant-ear sponge, long corkscrews of wire coral, and a few delicate colonies of black coral.

Divers sometimes miss the black corals because they are looking for colonies that are actually black. The name can be misleading; black corals,

F

D

E

G

including wire corals, get their color from pigments in the tissue of the polyps, which gives them muted hues of pink, green, and rusty brown rather than black.

Turtles are likely to be seen close to the wall here, and schooling bar jacks and horse-eye jacks are common in the blue water just off the edge of the wall.

*G. Sculptured slipper lobster, Parribacus antarcticus, can be spotted at night on Anchor Wall.*

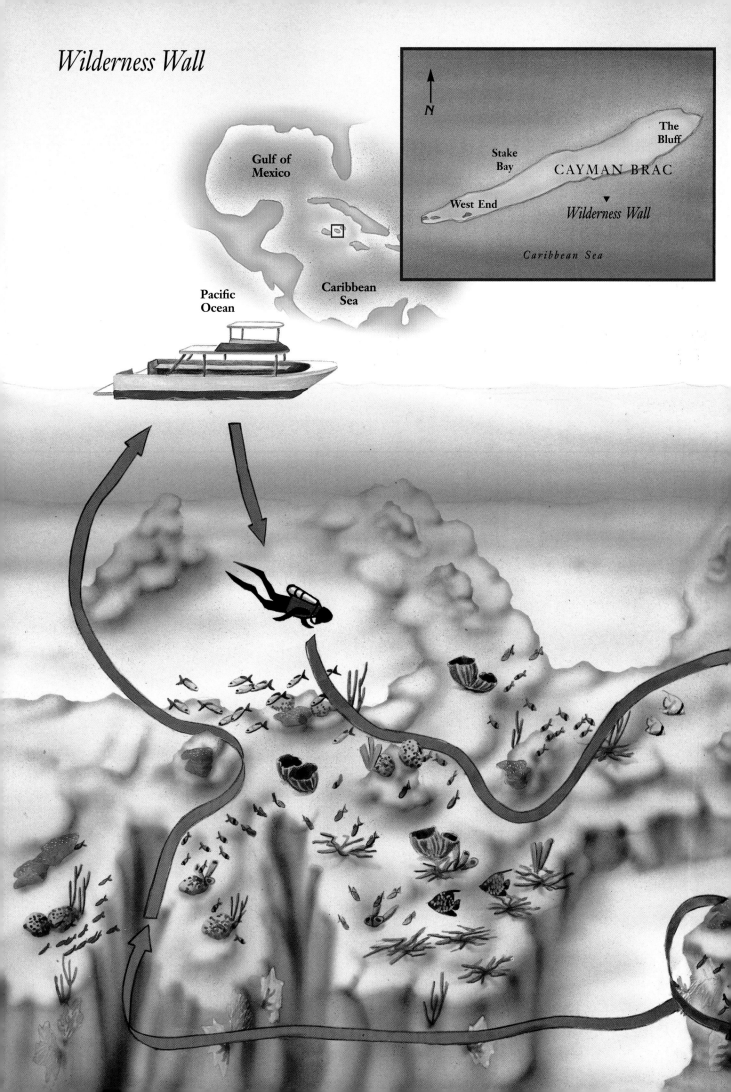

Wilderness Wall

Gulf of
Mexico

Pacific
Ocean

Caribbean
Sea

Stake
Bay

West End

The
Bluff

CAYMAN BRAC

Wilderness Wall

Caribbean Sea

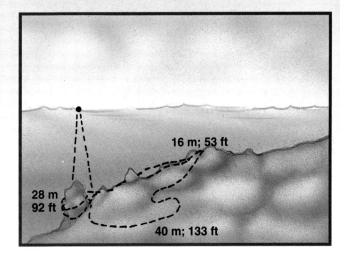

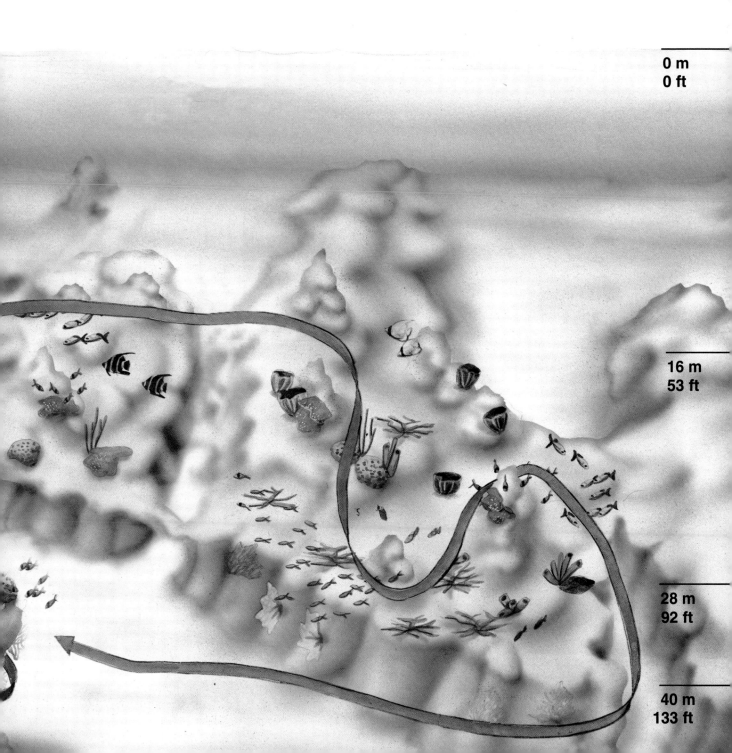

Sea Father Bay

N

16 m; 53 ft

28 m
92 ft

40 m; 133 ft

0 m
0 ft

16 m
53 ft

28 m
92 ft

40 m
133 ft

# Wilderness Wall

The wall is very convoluted at this site, providing many interesting canyons to explore.

Several nice pinnacles rise from the reef well back from the wall edge, and one prominent pinnacle is located off the face of the wall. The top of this pinnacle is at 85 or 90 feet (25 to 27 meters)

and is well covered with a mix of hard and soft corals. To the west of the pinnacle is a long spur with vertical sides that are cut inward in several places. These concave sections are filled with a large variety of sponges. Moose antler sponges grow in great looping branches, overlapping brown tube sponges and purple finger sponges. If you have a dive light, it will reveal splashes of bright red and yellow where encrusting sponges have plastered over any available hard surface. The great concentration of

*A. Vertical cuts in the face of Wilderness Wall provide interesting places to explore.*

*B. A tangle of rope sponges dangles from the underside of a coral ledge at Wilderness Wall.*

*C. A diver illuminates a delicate black coral colony at about 80 feet (24 meters) on Wilderness Wall.*

*D. Schools of horse-eye jacks frequently circle in the blue water off Wilderness Wall.*

*E. A diver follows the silvery reflections of a school of jacks.*

*F. In this close-up you can see a few schoolmasters,* Lutjanus apodus, *common inhabitants of Wilderness Wall.*

*G. A golden-phase coney,* Cephalopholis fulvus, *opens its mouth for a cleaner fish on Wilderness Wall.*

E

F

sponges beneath these ledges attracts a large population of fish and invertebrates. Four members of the angelfish family, rock beauties, French angels, gray angels, and queen angels, are especially well represented. Farther west are two more large spurs, a considerable distance apart but easily visible from one to the other. Watch your depth carefully if you decide to cross from tip to tip rather than contour around with the wall, because it is easy to go deeper than you intend without a bottom reference. The water column above the wall is a busy zone for reef fish feeding on tiny animals suspended in the water. Black durgon, Creole wrasse, blue chromis, and bar

G

jacks are usually present in large numbers, flitting back and forth in loose schools as they feed.

Silvery schools of horse-eye jacks are often seen here too, although they tend to circle in the blue water just past the edge of the wall. A slow, careful approach with a minimum of movement and gentle exhalations will let you approach the jacks without disturbing their school.

Wilderness Wall is located on Cayman Brac's south wall. The top of the wall starts at about 60 feet (18 meters). Visibility is normally 100 feet (30 meters) or more. Currents can range from none to strong, but are normally light to moderate.

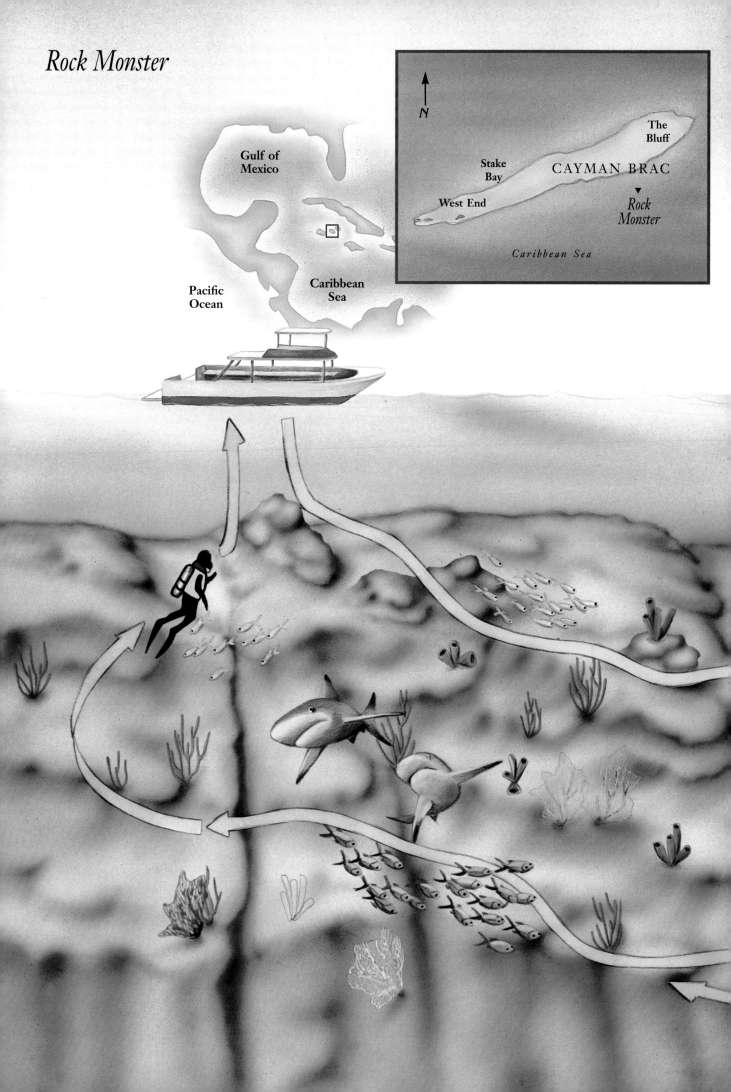

Rock Monster

Gulf of
Mexico

Pacific
Ocean

Caribbean
Sea

N

Stake
Bay

The
Bluff

CAYMAN BRAC

West End

Rock
Monster

Caribbean Sea

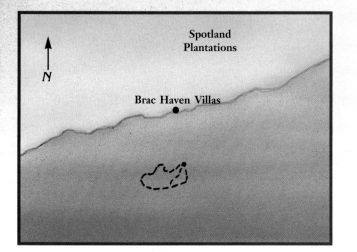

Spotland
Plantations

N

Brac Haven Villas

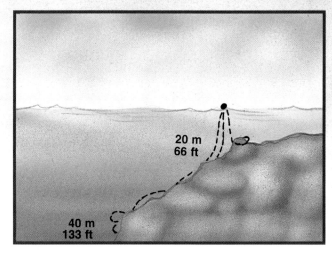

20 m
66 ft

40 m
133 ft

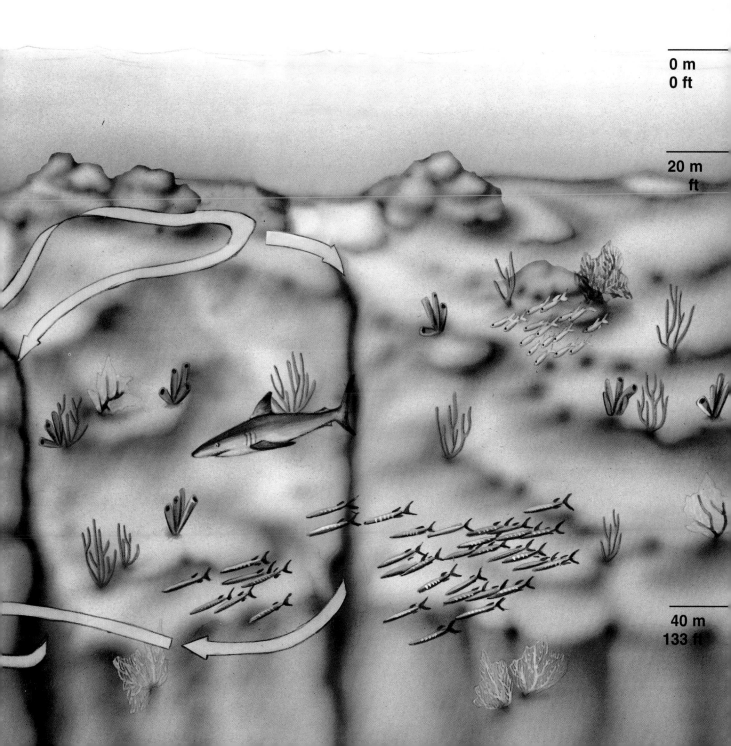

0 m
0 ft

20 m
ft

40 m
133 ft

# Rock Monster

I f you are staying on Cayman Brac and look out to see calm seas and bright sunshine along the south shore, begin to chant "Bluff Run!" Maybe your divemaster will take the hint and stage an expedition cruising along the south shore all the way to the east end of the island.

Not only is it a scenic boat ride, the dive sites are rarely visited and quite

D

*A. A diver's light illuminates deep-water gorgonians hanging from a grotto at Rock Monster.*

A

B

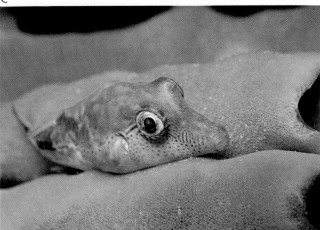

C

E

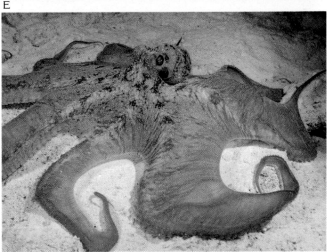

remarkable. Rock Monster, Son of Rock Monster, Bluff Wall, and Ken's Mountain are all viable destinations for any bluff run, and this description of Rock Monster fits the profile of the other sites as well. The wall here begins at about 60 feet (18 meters), but there are giant sand channels and canyons that cleave the substrate. The sand actually flows slowly across the wall, like a solid waterfall that is almost, but not quite, frozen in time. Some of the crevices are overgrown and

*B. Clear water and the lack of particles in suspension help divers take photos of schools of silvery fish like these horse-eye jacks, Caranx latus.*

*C. Well camouflaged on a sponge, the photographer found this sharpnose puffer, Canthigaster rostrata, at Rock Monster. D. Deep-water gor-*

F

provide swim-through tunnels exiting along the wall. Others may be open at the top but are winding and convoluted enough to provide a fascinating route to the drop-off. Many of the ledges are dripping with various rope and tube sponges, making this area a delight for wide-angle photographers. For some reason, however, these walls are not extravagantly populated with fish.

Of course, there is always the chance of seeing a pelagic, especially a blacktip shark, but the reef fish tend to be sparse. The main attraction is the stunning visibility, which often exceeds 150 feet (45 meters), and the dramatic terrain. Currents are moderate to strong.

I

*D. Deep-water gorgonian,* Iciligorgia schrammi, *and red rope sponge,* Aplysina cauliformis, *on the wall at Rock Monster. Divers must always be very careful when approaching these masterpieces.*

*E. It is quite unusual to find a Caribbean reef octopus,* Octopus briareus, *lying on the sandy bottom.*

*F. Along the reef divers can make many interesting discoveries like this*

*queen angelfish,* Holacanthus ciliaris.

*G. A green sea turtle at night leaves the shelter of the reef, going toward the open sea.*

*H. A spotted moray eel,* Gymnothorax moringa, *peeps out from its refuge, surrounded by many colorful marine forms.*

*I. A parrotfish settles in for the night along the reef at Rock Monster.*

# LITTLE CAYMAN

A

B

Located only about 7 miles (11 kilometers) from the tip of Cayman Brac and 86 miles (137 kilometers) northeast of Grand Cayman, Little Cayman for many years was the Cayman Islands' wilderness refuge. However, the island's legendary dive attractions have recently brought new development. Once there were only a couple of guest houses and small resorts; now there are five resorts and a variety of condominiums available for purchase or short-term rental.

A real estate boom of sorts has come to Little Cayman, and even though resort development is still small and tasteful, collectively it brings significantly more divers to the island. The island is just 9 miles (14.4 kilometers) long and barely 1 mile (1.6 kilometers) wide. Mostly flat, it has an elevation of 40 feet (12 meters).

A small but scenic nearby island known as Owen Island is a bird sanctuary with a lovely sand beach popular with Little Cayman visitors, and also occasionally for day dive boats from Cayman Brac giving divers something to do during surface intervals. If you visit, don't spoil this idyllic setting by leaving trash behind.

Most of the dive sites on Little Cayman are in one of the two main diving areas, Bloody Bay and Jackson Bight. On the following pages are descriptions of four dives at Jackson Bight and three at Bloody Bay.

C

*A. A DeHavilland Twin Otter picks up passengers on the grass at Edward Bodden Airfield on Little Cayman.*

*B. Peaceful beaches are one of Little Cayman's many natural attractions.*

*C. In this aerial view of the north coast of Little Cayman, you can see Bloody Bay and Jackson Bight.*

*D. Little Cayman waters are very rich in marine life; here is a mixed school of grunts and snappers along the reef edge at Three Fathom Wall.*

*E. Natural light and the photographer's strobe reflect on the white sandy bottom, illuminating the entrance to a cavern at Cumber's Caves, at approximately 50 feet (15 meters).*

# Magic Roundabout

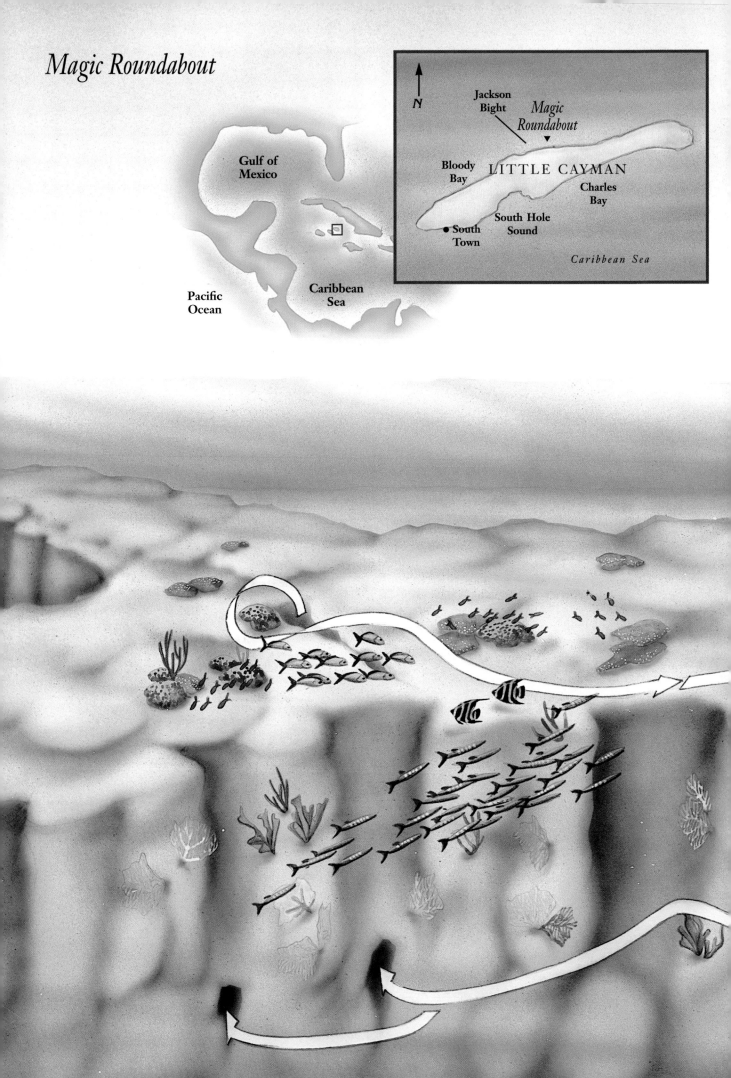

Jackson Bight

*Magic Roundabout*

Bloody Bay

LITTLE CAYMAN

Charles Bay

South Hole Sound

• South Town

*Caribbean Sea*

N

Gulf of Mexico

Pacific Ocean

Caribbean Sea

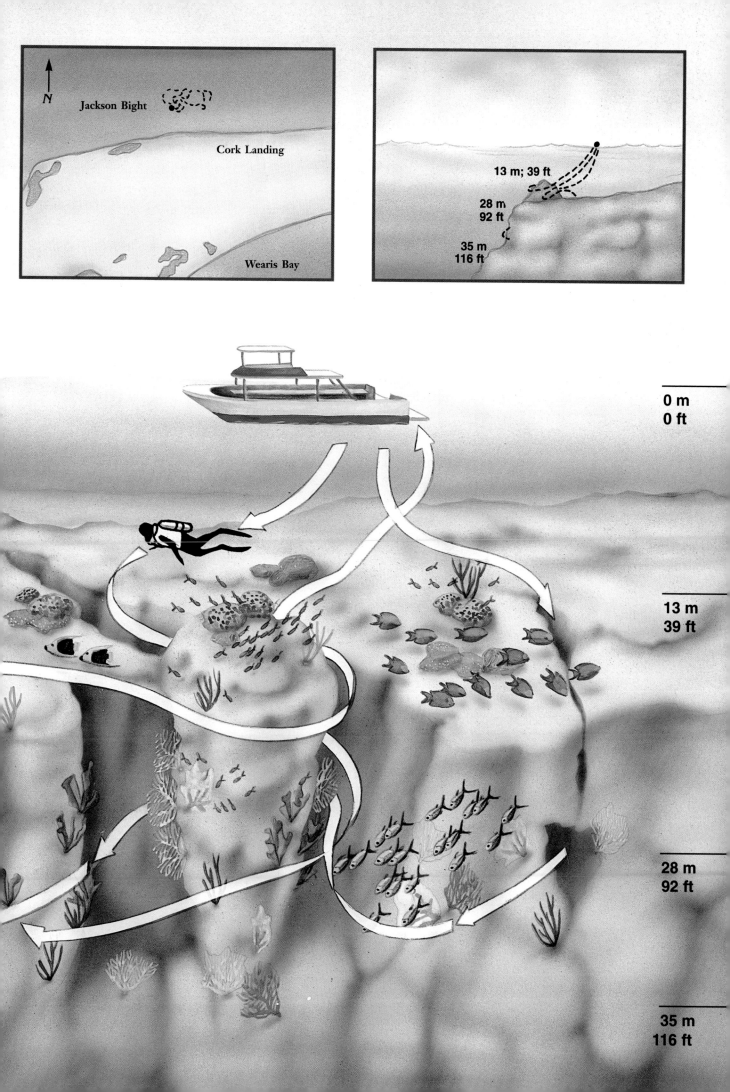

Jackson Bight

Cork Landing

Wearis Bay

N

13 m; 39 ft

28 m
92 ft

35 m
116 ft

0 m
0 ft

13 m
39 ft

28 m
92 ft

35 m
116 ft

A

# Magic Roundabout

The dive briefing for Magic Round-about will probably describe a pin-nacle, but don't be misled into looking for a distinct coral spire adjacent to the wall. The pinnacle is actually overgrown and connected to the wall at the top, which makes it easy to miss if you don't know which coral canyon to follow. Since it is very near the wall, it is hard to visually separate from other aspects of the wall when viewed from the

B

E

C

D

seaward side. Following an experienced dive guide may be the best bet for seeing the roundabout.

The pinnacle, or roundabout, is found at a depth of 70 to 120 feet (21 to 36 meters) and allows circumnavigation through a crevice rich with black coral species, rope sponges, and orange ele-phant-ear sponge formations. At the exit from the roundabout, the face of the wall is a vertical precipice. It probably doesn't matter whether a diver heads left or right once exiting the roundabout, for the level of decoration along the wall is similar for several hundred yards in either direction. The facets of the wall are fascinating, but there is actually a greater concentration of reef life in the shallows.

After a quick tour of the drop-off, most divers head for shallower waters. The combination of unique sand-dwelling species and a rich coral reef makes these areas of Jackson Bight a fish watcher's paradise. Blennies are particularly plentiful in the shallows, including the hard-to-find sailfin blenny, the yellow-headed diamond blenny, and the elusive dusky blenny. The shallow zone of Magic Roundabout is also a good place to see parrotfish in all the various stages of their life cycle. Because of the tendency of divers to want to spend time

in the shallows at the end of the dive, this is a perfect second dive, assuring an entertaining means to offgas at the end of the day.

*A. A diver cautiously moves close to a squirrelfish,* Holocentrus adscensionis, *at Magic Roundabout.*

*B. Several species of sponge fight for space on this promontory at Magic Roundabout.*

*C. Deep-water gorgonians,* Iciligorgia schrammi, *dominate the seascape at Magic Roundabout.*

*D. Rope sponges grow in abundance in the sheltered space beneath the overhangs at Magic Roundabout.*

*E. Tall mounds of giant star coral,* Montastrea cavernosa, *cap the edge of the reef at Magic Roundabout.*

*F. The sun burns brightly through the clear water, even at 100 feet (30 meters).*

*G. An Atlantic manta,* Manta birostris, *glides through the deep water at Magic Roundabout.*

*H. A queen parrotfish,* Scarus vetula, *rests protected by its mucous cocoon at night.*

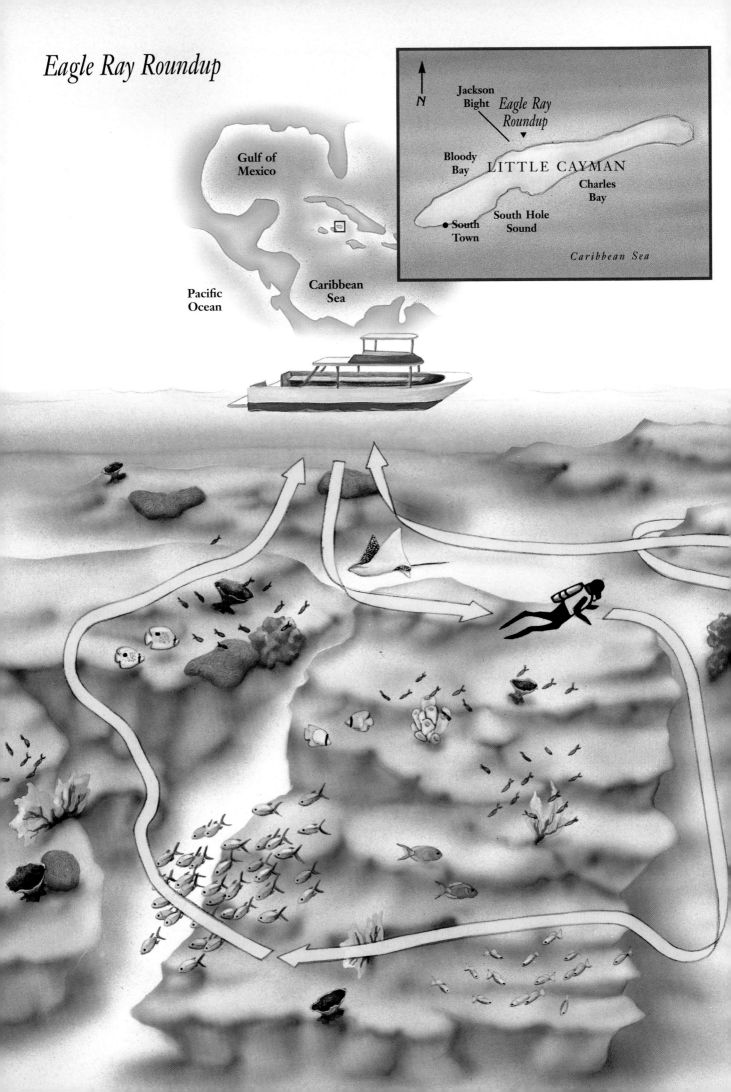

# Eagle Ray Roundup

Gulf of Mexico

Pacific Ocean

Caribbean Sea

N

Jackson Bight

*Eagle Ray Roundup*

Bloody Bay

LITTLE CAYMAN

Charles Bay

South Hole Sound

● South Town

*Caribbean Sea*

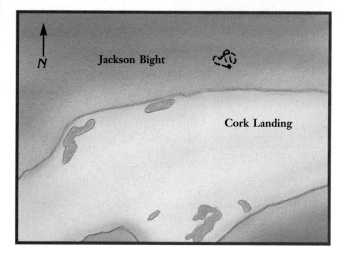

Jackson Bight

Cork Landing

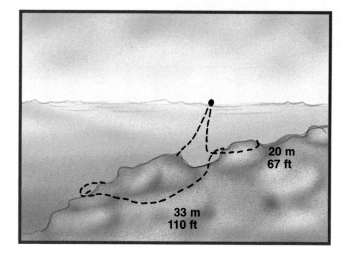

20 m
67 ft

33 m
110 ft

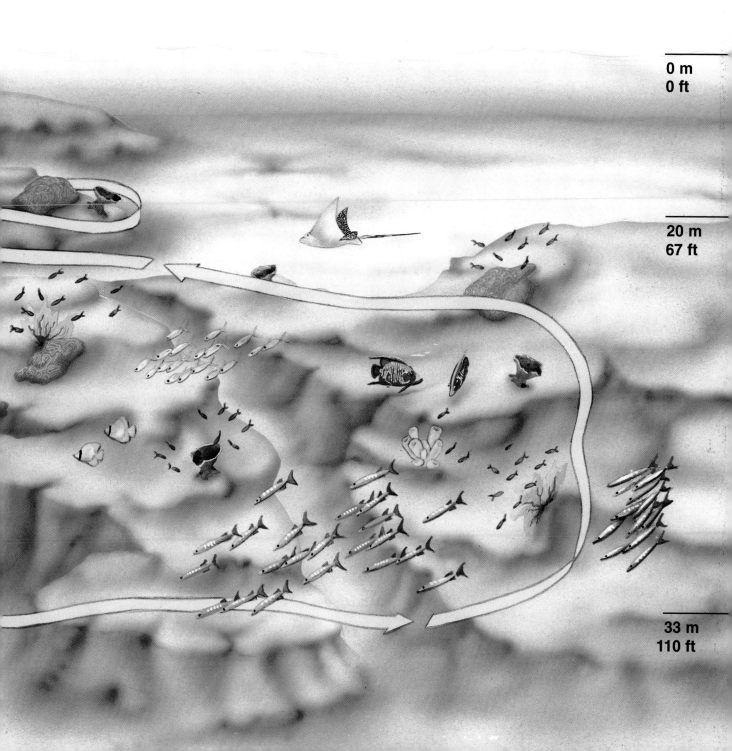

0 m
0 ft

20 m
67 ft

33 m
110 ft

# Eagle Ray Roundup

The mooring at Eagle Ray Roundup lies in a large sand arena where spotted eagle rays often come to dine on small crustaceans buried in the sand. Southern stingrays frequent the sandy plain for the same reason. Even nurse sharks have been observed preying on the queen conch here. In this bizarre feeding ritual, the nurse shark turns the conch over with its snout and then literally sucks the living conch out of its shell.

There must be more queen conchs than nurse sharks can eat, however, because the conchs seem defenseless, yet there are always plenty of them all along the sandy areas of Jackson Bight.

A shallow coral buttress spans the shoreward side of the sand, although the corals at the top are not as pristine as those in slightly deeper water, probably

*A. The diver follows a school of horse-eye jacks,* Caranx latus, *in the open water adjacent to the wall at Eagle Ray Roundup.*

*B. Star coral heads at Eagle display the "mushroom" shape of older colonies.*

A

C

due to the impact of storm surge. High-profile coral islets on the sand provide habitat for trumpetfish, angelfish, damselfish, and surgeonfish, and the lip of the wall attracts tiger grouper to numerous cleaning stations.

A large population of brown garden eels lives in slender burrows in the extensive sand flat ringed by the coral mounds. The encrusting growth along the wall at Eagle Ray is more sparse than is typical of many Jackson Bight sites, but

*C. A photographer takes aim at a strawberry vase sponge,* Mycale laxissima, *at Eagle Ray Roundup.*

*D. The diver has found a queen conch lying on the sandy bottom at Eagle Ray Roundup.*

*E. This was an easy shot because this tiger grouper,* Mycteroperca tigris, *was immobile at a cleaning station at Eagle Ray Roundup.*

there are still many colorful sponge and black coral colonies.

As is typical of most Jackson Bight sites, the visibility along the wall is generally excellent.

On average 100-foot (30-meter) visibility can be expected along the face of the drop-off, but there may be a turbid haze in the upper 15 to 20 feet (4.5 to 6 meters) of water, particularly on an outgoing tide. This can degrade water clarity on the shallow portions of the reef,

but aside from absorbing surface light, it has little effect on lateral visibility at depths greater than 50 feet (15 meters).

*F. A yellowtail snapper,* Ocyurus chrysurus, *hides from a photographer behind the barrels of a yellow tube sponge.*

*G. A spotted eagle ray,* Aetobatus narinari, *forages for invertebrates in the sand at Eagle Ray Roundup.*

# Cumber's Caves

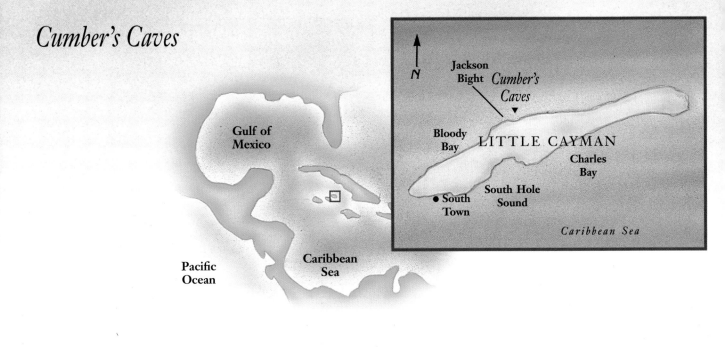

Gulf of
Mexico

Caribbean
Sea

Pacific
Ocean

Jackson
Bight
*Cumber's
Caves*
▼
Bloody
Bay
LITTLE CAYMAN
Charles
Bay
● South
Town
South Hole
Sound
*Caribbean Sea*

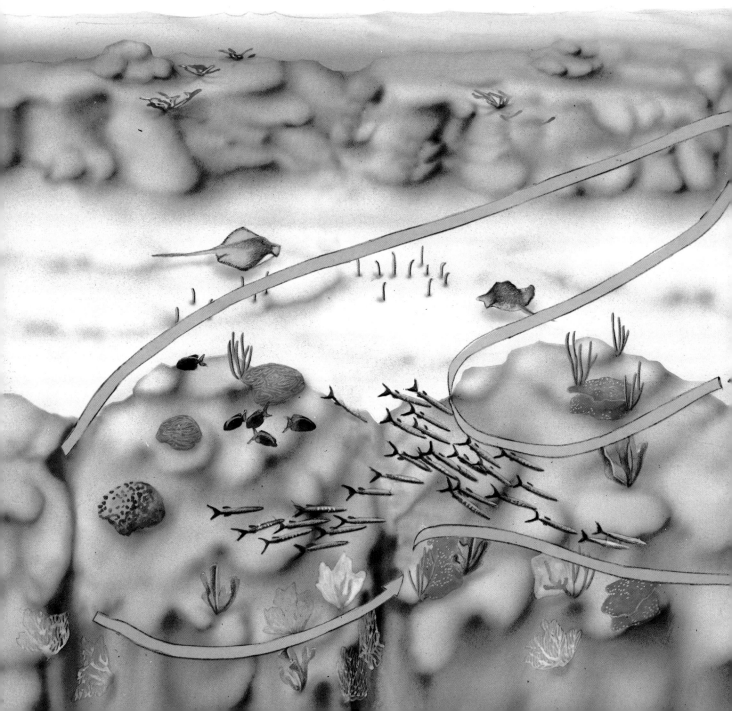

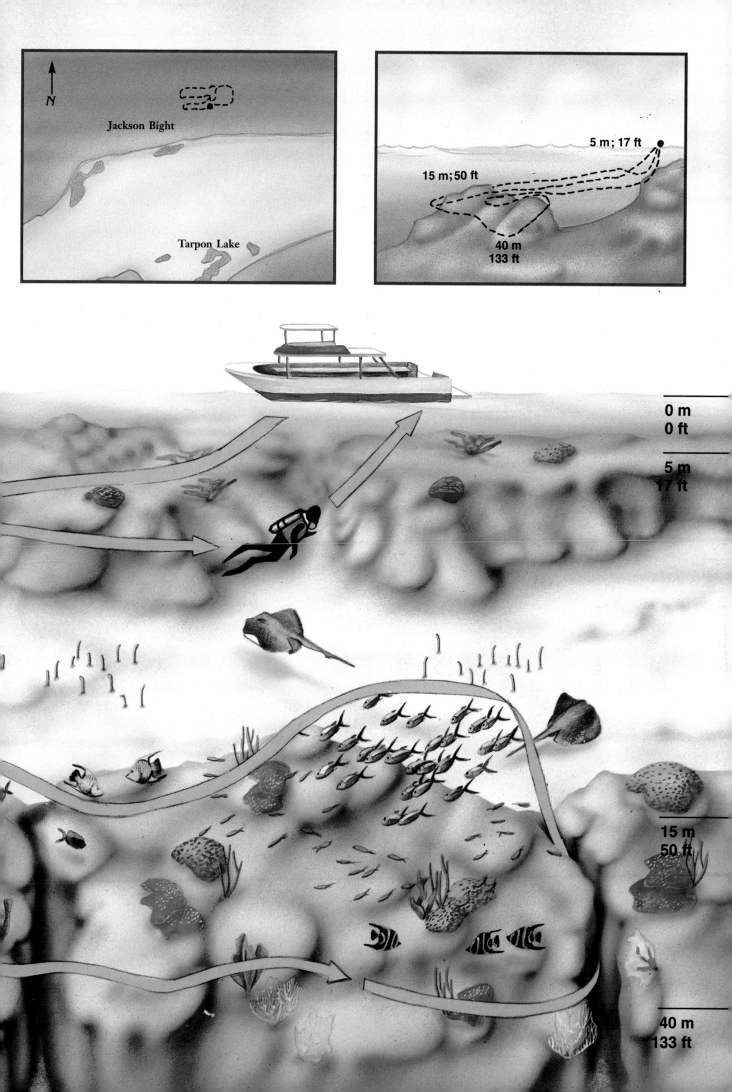

Jackson Bight

Tarpon Lake

5 m; 17 ft

15 m; 50 ft

40 m
133 ft

0 m
0 ft

5 m
17 ft

15 m
50 ft

40 m
133 ft

A

B

C

# Cumber's Caves

In the vicinity of Cumber's Caves, the structure of the wall is considerably different than at most other sites in the Caymans, but typical of the entire Jackson Bight area. A massive coral parapet has formed along the lip of the wall, with a broad sandy plain on the shoreward side.

The sand is inhabited by thousands of swaying garden eels. These shy creatures slide tail-first into their holes at the approach of a diver, but with patience you can watch them weave back and forth as they pluck their microscopic food from the water.

The sand plain is also the dining room of numerous southern stingrays, which search tirelessly for invertebrates hidden in the sand. When they find a likely prey, they literally suck it from the sand, bouncing up and down on the seafloor. Often a bar jack or coney hoping to pick up a free scrap will shadow one of the rays. These fish seem to regard the ray as their own and will vigorously fight off any other fish that tries to horn in on the action.

Cumber's Caves are unique because the small caves are comprised of fossilized calcium carbonate above and sand below. The roof of these caves essentially forms the top of the wall, and the undercut portion exits along the face of the wall at depths from 60 to 120 feet (18 to 36 meters). The caves probably originated as sand chutes cutting through the coral along the lip of the wall. The coral then gradually grew over the top of the chutes, changing them from valleys to caves.

The walls of the caves are quite smooth and unadorned in some places; in others there is a thick coating of sponges and considerable encrusting coral.

Cumber's Caves is located on the north side of Little Cayman, adjacent to Jackson Bight. Visibility is normally

D

E

F

about 100 feet (30 meters) along the wall, although the sandy area on the shallow side of the wall can become somewhat churned up by the outgoing tide or wind and resultant wave action.

*A. Divers approach the entrance to a cavern at Cumber's Caves; depth is approximately 50 feet (15 meters).*

*B. Deep-water gorgonians and a variety of tube sponges in a growth pattern typical of the deep environment at Cumber's Caves.*

G

*C. A diver is about to enter a cavern at Cumber's Caves, leading from the sandy bottom on the shallow side of the wall to the face of the wall.*

*D. A Nassau grouper, Epinephelus striatus, poses for the video camera.*

*E. French angelfish, Pomancanthus paru, can often be observed swimming in pairs.*

*F. A gray angelfish, Pomacanthus arcuatus, represents an easy find at Cumber's Caves.*

*G. Looking carefully at the sandy bottom, one can notice very shy animals: brown garden eels, Heteroconger halis.*

# Bus Stop

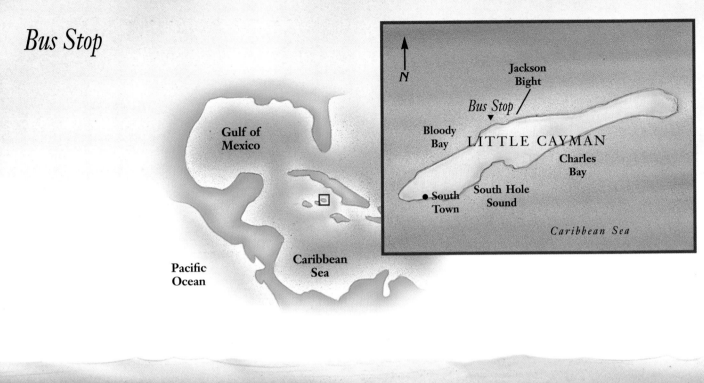

Gulf of Mexico

Pacific Ocean

Caribbean Sea

**Inset map:**

N

Jackson Bight

*Bus Stop*

Bloody Bay

LITTLE CAYMAN

Charles Bay

South Town

South Hole Sound

*Caribbean Sea*

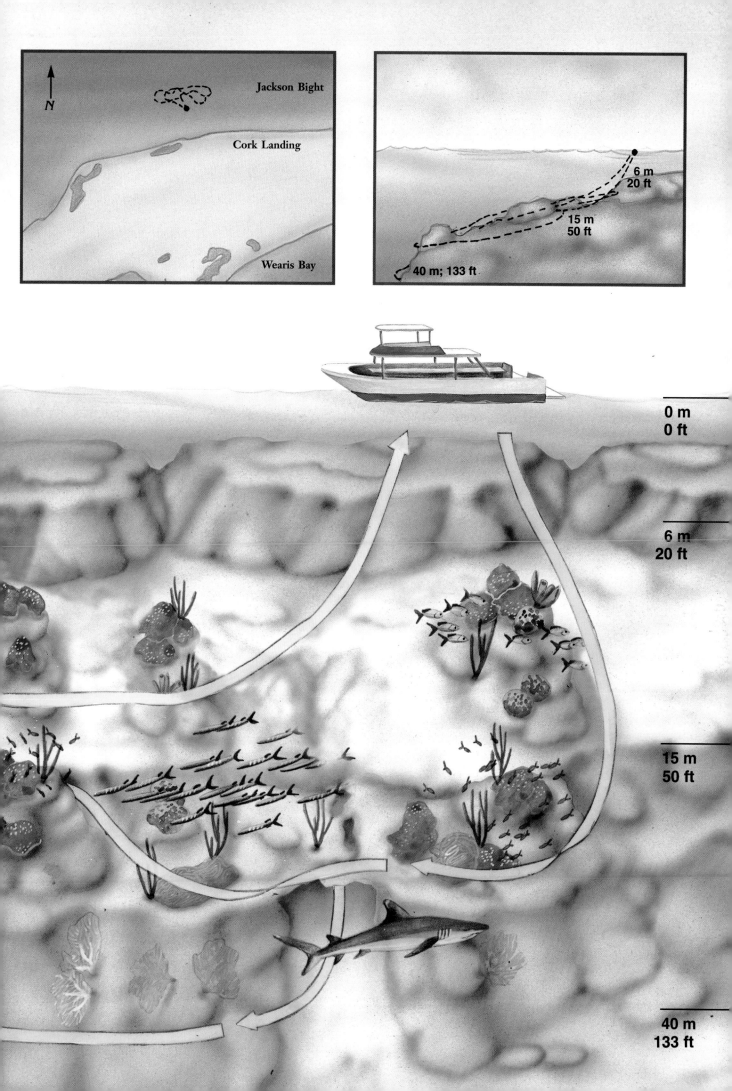

Jackson Bight

Cork Landing

Wearis Bay

N

6 m
20 ft

15 m
50 ft

40 m; 133 ft

0 m
0 ft

6 m
20 ft

15 m
50 ft

40 m
133 ft

# Bus Stop

A

B

A broken-down school bus on the shore near here gave the site its name, but it is no longer visible. This site offers a mini-wall at the shallow end of the reef, which falls away to rubble on the shoreward edge in typical Jackson Bight fashion. Several small coral islands rise to 30 feet (9 meters) from a broad sand "meadow" about 50 feet (15 meters) deep, with giant barrel sponges. The direction in which boats normally lie at this site provides easy

C

D

E

access to a giant swim-through tunnel that exits the wall at 80 feet (24 meters). Unlike some of the more claustrophobic tunnels elsewhere on this wall, this one is large enough for six divers side by side. Reef sharks frequently patrol the wall at Bus Stop. Divers sometimes see them approaching from the deep or paralleling the wall. Keep an eye to the blue water here, and you may be rewarded with a blacktip shark sighting. Excessive currents are uncommon here; in fact, most days are devoid of current. Visibility will be excellent unless big waves pound the shore and stir the sand into suspension even this far offshore.

F

A. A photographer frames a French angelfish, Pomacanthus paru, *against the blue water at Bus Stop.*

B. *The diver seems to be attracted by a brilliant red strawberry vase sponge,* Mycale laxissima, *at Bus Stop.*

C. *A huge star coral,* Montastrea annularis, *at Bus Stop shows its age by its size and the way it has become undercut and mushroom-shaped.*

D. *A large smooth brain coral colony,* Diplora strigosa, *can be observed at Bus Stop.*

G

I

H

E. *A Nassau grouper,* Epinephelus striatus, *swims behind a large gorgonian at Bus Stop.*

F. *Looking carefully at the sandy bottom, one can observe queen conch,* Strombus gigas.

G. *This nurse shark,* Ginglymostoma cirratum, *seems to be completely surrounded by a thick school of silversides.*

H. *Night dives at Bus Stop are quite common. During night dives, one can discover a completely different world and meet animals different from those of the day, like this Caribbean reef squid,* Sepioteuthis sepioidea.

I. *Colorful and rich coral promontories mark the sides of the sand chute.*

# Three Fathom Wall

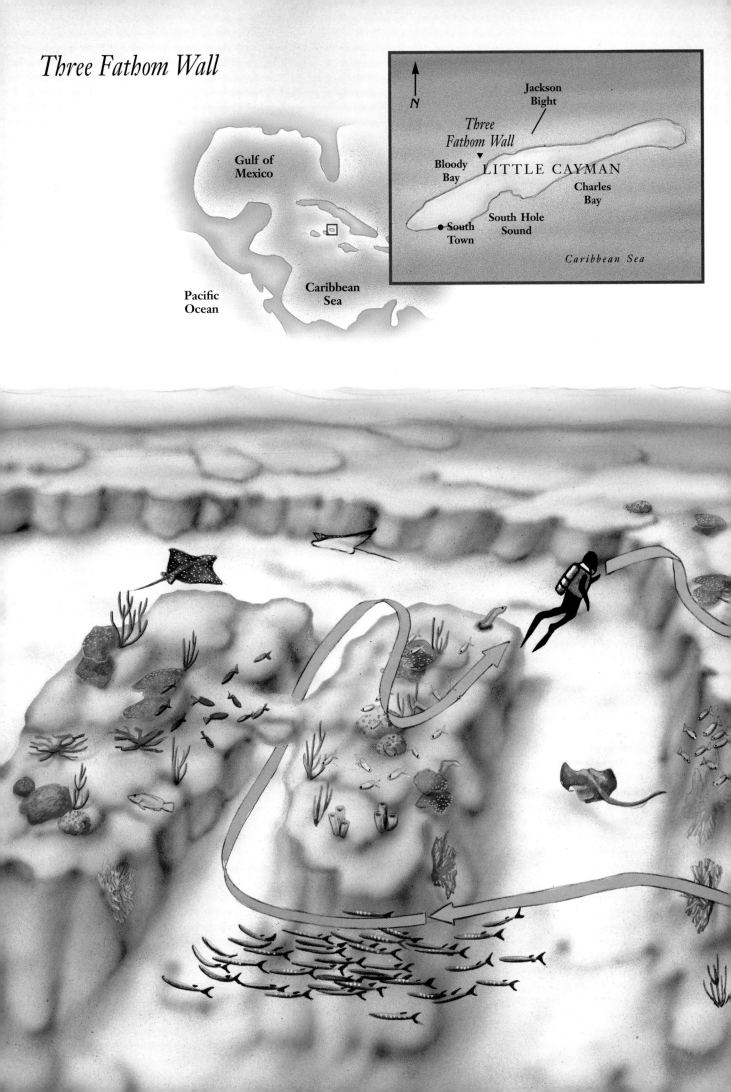

Gulf of
Mexico

Pacific
Ocean

Caribbean
Sea

### (inset map)

N

Jackson
Bight

Three
Fathom Wall

Bloody
Bay

LITTLE CAYMAN

Charles
Bay

● South
Town

South Hole
Sound

Caribbean Sea

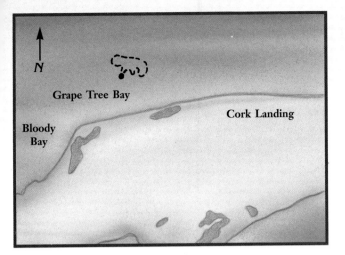

Bloody Bay

Grape Tree Bay

Cork Landing

N

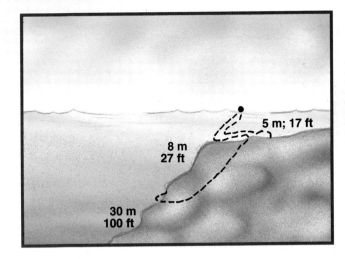

5 m; 17 ft

8 m
27 ft

30 m
100 ft

0 m
0 ft

5 m
17 ft

8 m
27 ft

30 m
100 ft

# Three Fathom Wall

During the Nikonos Shootout underwater photo competitions on Cayman Brac, the most requested dive site was not on Cayman Brac at all but on Little Cayman, at the Three Fathom Wall, also called the Mixing Bowl. Photographers knew this was an ideal place to find cooperative marine life, clear water, and shallow depths for ample bottom time.

This site gets one of its names, Three Fathom Wall, from the fact that the wall begins in only 18 feet (5 meters)

C

A

D

B

of water and the other, Mixing Bowl, because it is bisected by a large crevice separating the typical Bloody Bay Wall topography from that of Jackson Bight, mixing the two environments. Usually the boat lies to the west of the mooring, providing easy access to the shallow wall. Swimming east will bring you to the face of the crevice, often crowded with schools of snappers and grunts. For some reason the grunts here are far more tolerant of a diver's approach than at other sites noted for their schooling grunts like End of Island, Fishery, or even Grunt Valley. If you watch closely, you may see tiny Pederson cleaner shrimp dancing over the grunts and even inside

A. A southern stingray, Dasyatis americana, *hides in the sand at Three Fathom Wall.*

B. Mixed school of grunts and snappers along the reef edge.

C. A Nassau grouper, Epinephelus striatus, *greets a diver at Three Fathom Wall.*

D. Schoolmasters, Lutjanus apodus, *hover over the mouth of a large sponge.*

their mouths as they clean the fish of ectoparasites.

The shallow reef is so good some divers may never make it to the wall, but those who do find the large sponges and black corals typical of the Bloody Bay Wall. On the Jackson Bight side of the cleft, green morays often hide in coral recesses and southern stingrays prowl the sand flats.

Visibility along the wall is typically 100 feet (30 meters) or more, but the shallow areas of the reef, particularly in the hardpan, are more murky, especially when the seas are rough or during out-going tides.

F

E

G

H
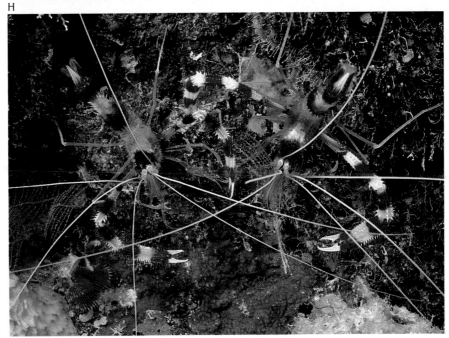

E. Deep-water gorgonians and sponges grow profusely on the deeper sections of Three Fathom Wall.

F. Mixed schools of grunts in the protection of a large mound of star coral, Montastrea annularis.

G. A dense school of grunts catches the eye of a photographer.

H. Banded coral shrimp, Stenopus hispidus, at Three Fathom Wall.

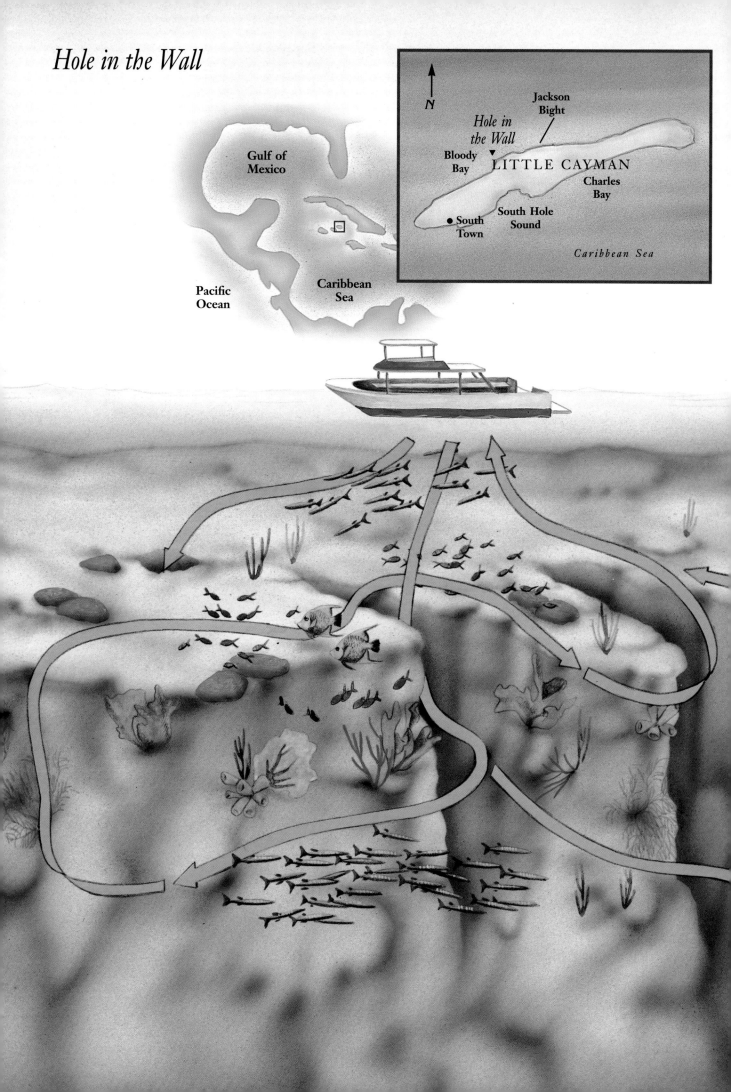

# Hole in the Wall

**Gulf of Mexico**

**Pacific Ocean**

**Caribbean Sea**

N

*Hole in the Wall*

Jackson Bight

Bloody Bay

LITTLE CAYMAN

Charles Bay

South Town

South Hole Sound

*Caribbean Sea*

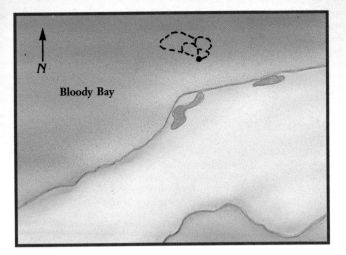

Bloody Bay

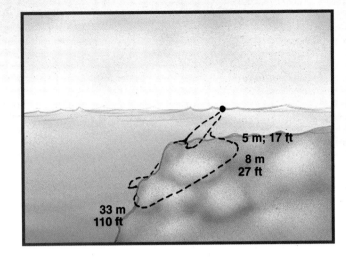

5 m; 17 ft

8 m
27 ft

33 m
110 ft

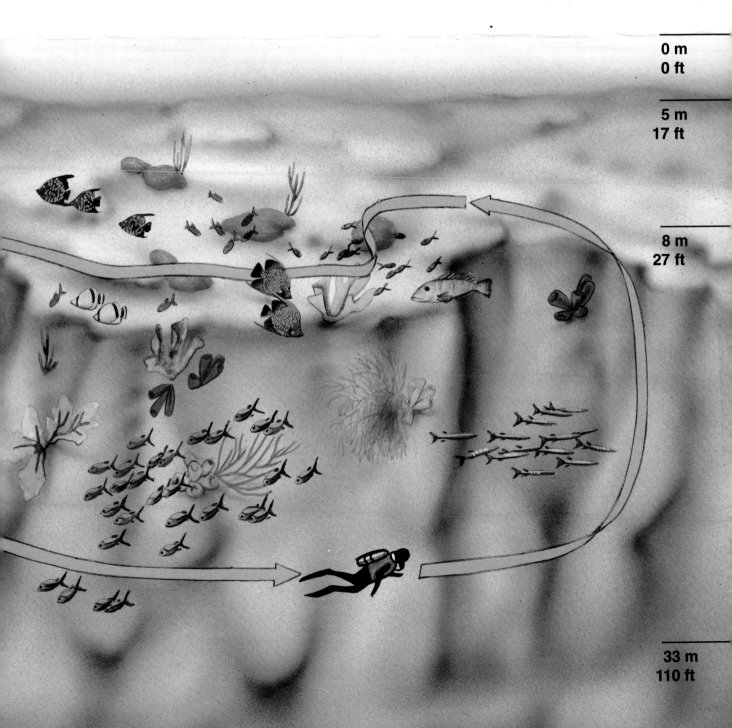

0 m
0 ft

5 m
17 ft

8 m
27 ft

33 m
110 ft

# Hole in the Wall

*A. The deeper sections of Hole in the Wall feature prolific growths of deep-water gorgonians and a variety of sponges.*

*B. A diver is silhouetted against the sun outside Hole in the Wall.*

*C. Divers prepare to explore one of the deep vertical cuts at Hole in the Wall.*

C

idway along the expanse of Bloody Bay Wall is an interesting site notable for a large open passageway that leads through a long, convoluted tunnel, finally exiting along the vertical wall at about 65 feet (20 meters). Like most of Bloody Bay, the wall starts at about 25 feet (7.5 meters) and drops precipitously to 6,000 feet (1,800 meters). Responsible divers stop far short of that mark, much closer to 100 feet (30 meters).

A

B

D

This sheer drop can induce vertigo in some divers, but the more common emotion is ecstasy, particularly when viewing the elaborate coral and sponge life typical along this wall.

Large orange elephant-ear sponges are common here, along with tube sponges, bushy black corals, and wire corals.

These dives are perfect for multi-level dives with computers. Begin this dive at the deepest point in your dive plan and gradually work back up the

*D. A Nassau grouper, Epinephelus striatus, amid brown tube sponges at Hole in the Wall.*

wall, stopping to take pictures or explore all along the way.

The reef crest is the ideal place to finish the dive, since it is not only shallow, but a far more entertaining environment than hanging on a line in the midwater during a safety stop.

Numerous cleaning stations permit divers to get close to the normally more reticent fish species like the tiger grouper. Squirrelfish are found throughout the shallow reef and angelfish roam in search of a likely sponge to nibble.

Small squadrons of Caribbean reef squid are sometimes seen in the shallow water over the reef, and Caribbean reef octopus can be seen on the bottom. Both of these animals possess an extraordinary ability to change color and texture, making them fascinating creatures to watch at close quarters. Beneath the boat it is not unusual to have a school of horse-eye jacks or barracuda congregate. They seem to like the shadow of the boat, probably because it helps them hide their silhouette from potential prey.

The whole expanse of Bloody Bay Wall is vertical in nature, but different areas offer significantly different concentrations of decoration.

The sponge growth from 70 to 120 feet (21 to 36 meters) along Hole in the Wall is quite inspiring, and the brilliant red, yellow, and orange hues of the filter feeders provide stunning contrast to the electric blue of the sea.

E. *A Nassau grouper nestles close to a common gorgonian,* Gorgonia ventalina, *at Hole in the Wall.*

F. *Horse-eye jacks,* Caranx latus, *school in the open water adjacent to the wall at Hole in the Wall.*

G. *The photographer has discovered this* coney, Cephalopholis fulvus, *at night along the reef wall at Hole in the Wall.*

# Chimney (Randy's Gazebo)

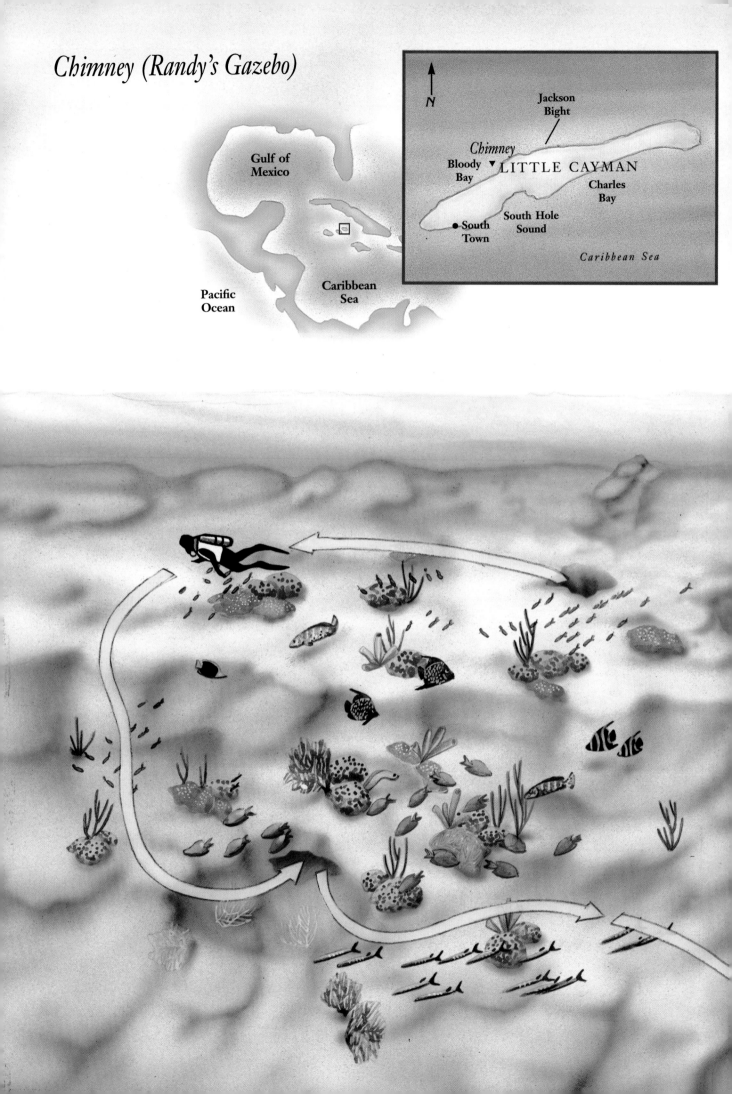

Jackson Bight

Chimney

Bloody Bay

LITTLE CAYMAN

Charles Bay

South Hole Sound

South Town

Caribbean Sea

Gulf of Mexico

Pacific Ocean

Caribbean Sea

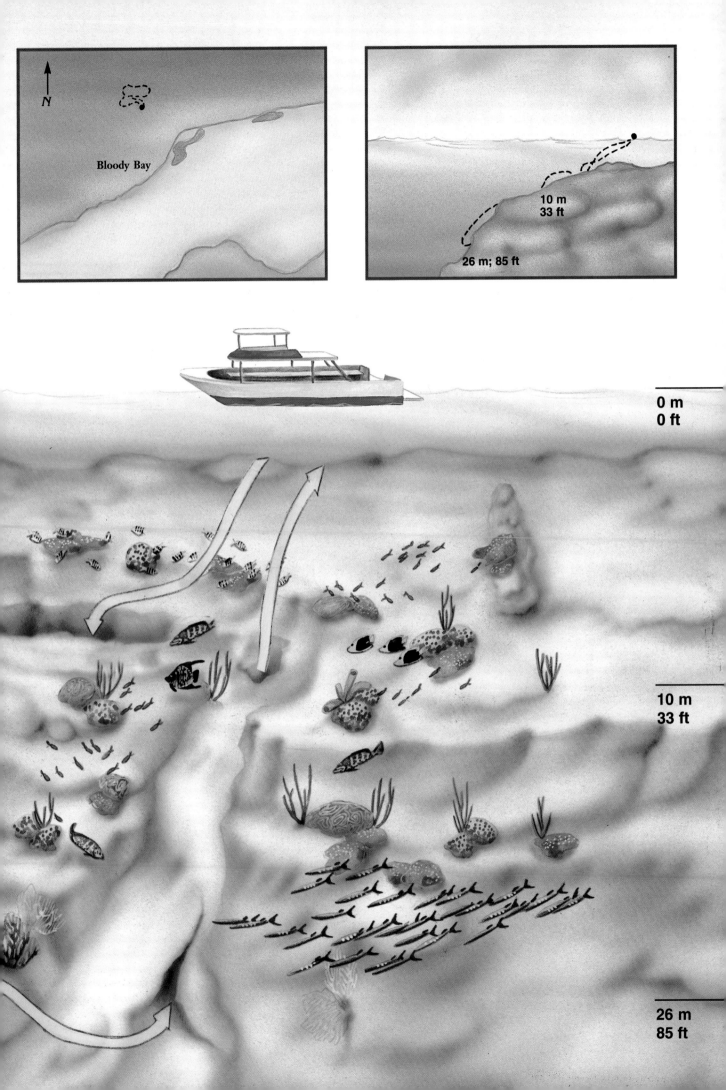

Bloody Bay

N

10 m
33 ft

26 m; 85 ft

0 m
0 ft

10 m
33 ft

26 m
85 ft

# Chimney (Randy's Gazebo)

M any Cayman dive sites have more than one name, since choosing the name has always been the prerogative of the dive operator. Hole in the Wall is also known as Marilyn's Cut; Chimney's alter ego is Randy's Gazebo. By whatever name, Chimney is a great dive. Almost directly seaward of the mooring line is a large opening in the shallow seafloor, which leads to a tunnel

*A. Sunrays show the diver's silhouette against the Chimney entrance.*

*B. Wide-angle photo opportunities abound at Chimney.*

*C. Squirrelfish,* Holocentrus adscensionis, *finds shelter among the barrels of a yellow tube sponge.*

*D. Lush soft corals, like deep-water gorgonians, combine with clusters of sponges to fill every possible space on the deep promontories at Chimney.*

exiting in a crevice, which then leads to the vertical wall. Confused? Don't be. It's actually a very easy swim-through and only one of many ways to enjoy this gorgeous vertical wall. Cooperative creatures seem to be a staple of Chimney; Nassau groupers and hawksbill turtles can be encountered at any depth, perhaps because of the extensive habitat available to animals at the Chimney. Everywhere you look there are sponges and corals, all providing shelter, food, or both for a variety of marine life. Coneys can be seen in all three color phases here—bright yellow with blue spots, reddish brown with blue spots, and a bicolor phase of red and white with blue spots. Another reason so many of the fish are so friendly is because they were at one time extensively fed along these Bloody Bay Wall sites. There is far less fish feeding going on today as divers become more aware of the problems inherent in providing marine life food not normal to its diet. It can make fish ill, or more significantly, desensitize them to danger from hook-

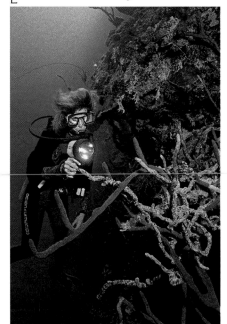

and-line anglers. There is yet another reason not to feed the fish—it can make them quite aggressive. Divemasters who have worked Little Cayman still tell tales of the grouper and horse-eye jacks that sometimes took a bit of diver flesh along with the proffered ballyhoo. The fish are now very friendly. You can speculate it's because of some Zen telepathy whereby you've communicated your benign intent. A less romantic notion is that the large grouper who poses for your camera is most likely expecting a reward.

*E. The photographer's strobe brings out the vivid colors of a tangle of rope sponges deep on the wall.*

*F. Nassau groupesr,* Epinephelus striatus, *can be observed at Chimney.*

*G. White grunts,* Haemulon plumieri, *shine thanks to the photographer's strobe.*

# INHABITANTS OF THE CAYMAN WATERS

Protected by the arc of the southern coast of the large island of nearby Cuba and by the tip of the Yucatan Peninsula, and lapped by the great swirls of northward-flowing warm current, the Cayman Islands are one of the scuba diving jewels of the real Caribbean Sea, which is something a little more particular than the generic geographical area usually associated with the term "Caribbean."

Surrounded by shallow waters that facilitate diving from the shore, the Caymans are the highest part of the ocean trench named after the islands and which, at Bartlett Deep, reaches a depth of 24,960 feet (7,488 meters).

These few notes, hardly sufficient to describe the Cayman Islands from an oceanographic point of view, are still enough to explain their popularity in the world of scuba diving. Their interest goes far beyond spending unforgettable hours in the company of the most famous rays in the world, found in Stingray City and Grand Cayman.

Exposed to the winds to varying degrees so that dives can be made in almost any weather condition, the Caymans are surrounded by extremely healthy coral reefs despite the huge number of divers that visit them each year. This is because of the high number of diving areas available in these incredibly limpid waters.

The seabed is not dissimilar to that in other parts of the Caribbean; large gorgonians and sponges, especially blood red sponges, seem to dominate everything in certain sections of the coast. Variety in the shoals is to be found around all three islands—Grand Cayman, Little Cayman, and Cayman Brac—as is their distinctive feature, sea walls that plunge over 900 feet (270 meters) and are home to all kinds of Caribbean organisms, distributed according to their environmental requirements.

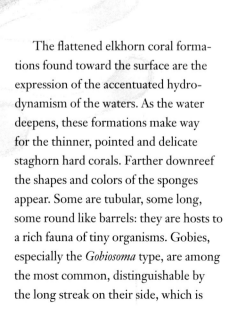

The flattened elkhorn coral formations found toward the surface are the expression of the accentuated hydrodynamism of the waters. As the water deepens, these formations make way for the thinner, pointed and delicate staghorn hard corals. Farther downreef the shapes and colors of the sponges appear. Some are tubular, some long, some round like barrels: they are hosts to a rich fauna of tiny organisms. Gobies, especially the *Gobiosoma* type, are among the most common, distinguishable by the long streak on their side, which is sometimes electric blue, yellow, or whitish. These gobies, also frequently found among the coral formations, sometimes come together in large numbers and create highly appreciated "cleaning stations"; they act like cleaner fish and attract many species in need of such a service.

Gorgonians rise next to the sponges and coral, both the purple ones shaped like compact fans and those found in deep water (Iciligorgia schrammi), also fan-shaped but reddish brown and with sparser ramifications.

Darting among them are rays, breams, wrasses of every color, but particularly the common blue-headed rainbow wrasse (Thalassoma bifasciatum), or the purple wrasse (Clepticus parrae). The company of fish includes the strange hamlet (the commonest is the indigo hamlet, Hypoplectrus indigo), triggerfish, surgeonfish (such as the blue surgeonfish, which is yellow when young, an oddity among fish), and the variously colored parrotfish, butterflyfish, and angelfish.

The most beautiful angelfish must be the queen angelfish (Holacanthus ciliaris) while the gray angelfish (Pomacanthus arcuatus), which is nearly always seen in pairs, depends on its size to attract the diver's attention.

Continuing this ideal dive among the reefs of the Cayman Islands, it is impossible not to note how the bottom is often intersected by deep, long ravines and canyons stretching in every direction, often merging.

Moving through this maze means passing through festoons of black coral, deep-water gorgonians, and sponges and swimming among other triggerfish, surgeonfish, or shoals of snappers or grunts that move in a dense pack under the watchful eye of a large grouper.

Moving slowly and carefully so as not to damage the delicate organisms on the sea walls, it is advisable to keep an eye on the cracks and recesses from where the red soldierfish and squirrelfish peep out.

Here you may see any of the many species of Caribbean moray eels, from the large green moray eel to the goldtailed eel. In the underwater caves and wide, poorly illuminated recesses, there will certainly be densely packed shoals of silversides that, thinking themselves safe, let the diver approach closer than other fish.

Lower down, the rock wall ends in wide flat paths and arenas that slowly fill with the coral sand excreted by the parrotfish as a subproduct of their strange feeding habits.

Here other forms of life are to be seen. Stingrays, skates, eagle rays, and nurse sharks are not rare, nor are the busy mullet, lizardfish, garden eels, mimetic turbot, gobies, and the similar Opistagnatus, the most attractive of which is certainly the yellow-headed variety, which should be approached with caution so that it does not retreat into its hiding place.

On the external wall of the reef, it is possible to observe invertebrates, many of which make up for their small size with brilliant colors. The dazzling masses of sea squirts, nudibranchs, mollusks, and gastropods are some of the favorite subjects of divers equipped with an underwater camera and macro lenses able to reveal the microscopic and mimetic

shrimps associated with anemones. Crustaceans equally worthy of attention are the cleaner shrimps (Stenopus and Lysmata), who are happy to offer their services to divers who are prepared to stay still long enough.

Also found are echinoderms like sea urchins, starfish, crinoids, and sea cucumbers, which, despite receiving varying degrees of divers' attention, are still popular—perhaps because they are easily recognized.

Before ending this dive, it is worth dedicating a little time to what can be seen in water away from the reef.

There may be silvery tarpon and various species of carangids, from the common Caranx latus to the rarest, which may unexpectedly open ranks to reveal the disquieting, but innocuous, presence of a large barracuda or a group of majestic manta rays.

As for sharks, they are certainly present, but regardless of their attraction to the Cayman Islands, there is so much to see that no diver would feel cheated if he only saw them from a distance or not at all.

# The Invertebrates

## Tube sponge
*Aplysina archeri*

Large sponge with long tubular formations that at times branch out from a common base. The tubes are soft and oscillate in the current. Colors vary from gray to violet on the outside, while they are generally whitish on the inside. Quite common, they grow on the deepest parts of the reef wall. They measure up to 60 inches (1.5 meters) long.

## Azure vase sponge
*Callyspongia plicifera*

A light blue sponge with pink shading; it has a triangular vase section with a narrow base and frayed edge opening. The surface is distinguished by variously formed raised ribbing. Such sponges grow singly or in groups of two or three along reef walls. They often host organisms such as small brittle stars, crustaceans or fish. They grow up to 20 inches (50 centimeters) long.

## Star coral
*Montastrea annularis*

Massive hard coral that looks like a lump on the seabed. Its surface is dotted with small raised corallites and subtle ribbing. Its colors vary from green to brownish yellow. The polyps are generally retracted during the day. This may be the dominant coral in some areas in depths from 30 to 90 feet (9 to 27 meters).

## Upside-down jellyfish
*Cassiopea frondosa*

A jellyfish that is easily recognized by its curious habit of resting on the sandy or plant-covered seabed with its tentacles trailing upward. If it is picked up, it begins swimming again like a normal jellyfish for a time before returning to the bottom. The tentacles are variously colored, as they contain symbiont microalgae from which the creature gains part of its nourishment. It measures up to 12 inches (30 centimeters) across.

## Finger coral
*Porites porites*

Colonies of this hard coral form stocky ramifications covered by large corallites and widened at the tips. Its coloring varies from beige to yellowish brown to purple. This species is quite tough and can have colonies with different appearances, depending on the depth of water and exposure to the waves. The colonies can exceed 39 inches (99 centimeters) in width.

## Elkhorn coral
*Acropora palmata*

Colonies of this hard coral are distinguished by their flattened ramifications, which branch out from a common base, parallel to the direction of the waves. The surface is sprinkled with small tubular corallites from which polyps extend at night. They are brown or yellowish brown with the tips lighter in color. This coral prefers shallow water and can exceed 66 inches (168 centimeters) in height.

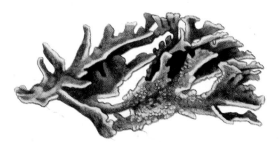

## Common Caribbean gorgonian
*Gorgonia ventalina*

Typical seafans are very dense and supported by large ramifications. The fans are flexible and wave with the water movement. Generally purple, they grow on external reefs or on isolated blocks of coral, and can reach 66 inches (168 centimeters) in height.

## Giant anemone
*Condylactis gigantea* ▶

A large sea anemone with long tentacles that end in a rounded flat tip, generally a purplish mauve color. If disturbed, it can retract its tentacles until it seems almost globular. Shrimp, small crabs, and butterflyfish are often found with this anemone. The tentacles can be slightly irritating to humans. It measures up to 12 inches (30 centimeters) in diameter.

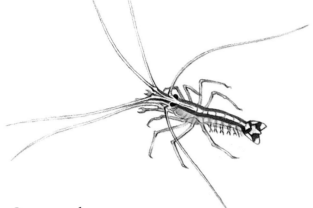

## Queen conch
*Strombus gigas* ▶

Gastropod mollusk with a large and projecting shell similar to a helmet with sturdy bulges. When the creature moves, it is possible to see its long proboscis and eyes at the end of retractable stalks. When necessary, the mollusk can retract inside its shell and close the door with a large operculum. It frequently lives on sandy seabeds that are rich with eelgrass. About 10 to 12 inches (25 to 30 centimeters) long.

◀ ## Cleaner shrimp
*Lysmata grabhami*

A typical small cleaner shrimp recognized by its reddish coloring and white stripe along its back and sides. Long white antennae stick out to the front, which the shrimp uses to signal its presence to fish that want to be cleaned of parasites. It lives in the cracks of the reef or near sponges. If approached carefully, it may crawl onto the diver's fingers. About 2 to 3 inches (5 to 7 centimeters) long.

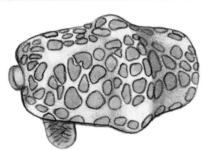

## Cushion starfish
*Oreaster reticulatus*

Solid, robust starfish with protruding, triangular arms and dark spines on its surface that form a geometric square and triangular mesh. It lives on sandy and detrital beds. Up to 16 inches (40 centimeters) in diameter. ▶

◀ ## Flamingo tongue
*Ciphoma gibbosum*

Gastropod mollusk usually found with seafans, on which it acts as a parasite, feeding from the seafan's polyps. The shell is shiny like a cowry shell but rarely seen, as it is covered by its expandable cloak, distinguished by roundish spots. Up to 1 inch (2.5 centimeters) long.

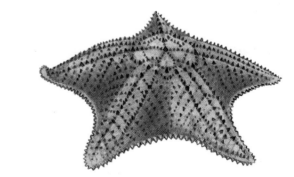

◀ ## Blue sea squirt
*Clavelina puertosecensis*

This sea squirt lives in colonies and is generally blue. Individuals are easy to distinguish and have siphons edged with white. They settle on reefs near sponges or in places where there are weak currents, which help them feed by filtration. Individual sea squirts measure less than ¾ inch (2 centimeters), but a colony reaches up to 6 inches (15 centimeters) in diameter.

# The Fishes

▼ **Nurse shark**
*Ginglymostoma cirratum*

Straight body flattened ventrally, with dorsal fins rather close together. Its mouth is small, ventral, and armed with a pair of short barbels. Yellowish gray in color. It lives on sandy seabeds among the reefs, sheltered by large corals and caves. Up to 12.5 feet (4 meters) in length. Common from Rhode Island to Brazil.

## TORPEDINIDAE FAMILY

**Lesser electric ray**
*Narcine brasiliensis*

The anterior portion of this ray is disk-shaped, narrowing to a medium-length tail surmounted by two dorsal fins. Its eyes are in a dorsal position. The ray's two bean-shaped electric organs, located at the side of its head, can be seen against the light. Its color varies from gray to reddish, with a few round spots. It lives on sandy seabeds to a depth of 90 to 120 feet (27 to 36 meters), and is up to 18 inches (.5 meters) in length. Its shock is weak and not dangerous to humans. Common from the Caribbean to Argentina.

## DASYATIDAE FAMILY

◀ **Southern stingray**
*Dasyatis americana*

Ray with more or less rhomboid body, with snout and tips of the pectoral fins slightly pointed. A row of tubercules runs down the center of the back. The anterior portion of the tail has a long pointed spine. When it rests on the seafloor, it tends to bury itself in the sand. Adults are blackish gray, while young individuals are lighter in color. Up to 4.5 feet (1.5 meters) wide. Common from New Jersey to Brazil.

## MOBULIDAE FAMILY

**Manta ray**
*Manta birostris*

This is certainly the best known representative of the rays, easily recognizable by its large pectoral fins, transformed into wings. The mobile cephalic fins that the manta uses to convey plankton into its mouth are also characteristic. It can often be observed in small groups swimming near the surface, where it allows the tips of its wings to emerge from the water. Its back is black, while its underside is pure white with black spots. May reach 20 feet (6 meters) in width.

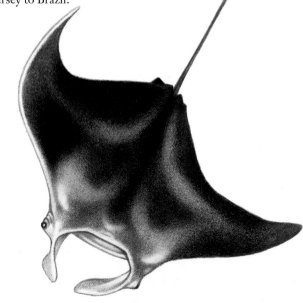

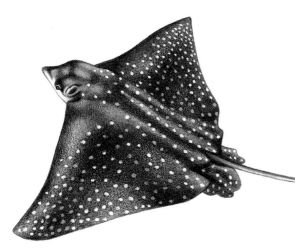

## MYLIOBATIDAE FAMILY

### Spotted eagle ray
*Aetobatus narinari*

Ray with a lozenge-shaped body and large pointed wings. Its head is pointed and convex. The tail is almost three times as long as the body, with jagged spines. The dorsal area is dark, with numerous light spots. It lives among the deep channels of the reef near sandy seabeds. Up to 7.5 feet (2.25 meters) in size. Common in circumtropical waters.

## MURAENIDAE FAMILY

### Green moray eel
*Gymnothorax funebris*

This moray is easily recognizable by its more or less uniformly dark green color. It is nocturnal, taking refuge during the day in the crevices of the reef, even at shallow depths, where it can easily be approached. It may attack if excessively disturbed. Up to 7 feet (2 meters) in length. Common from Florida to Brazil.

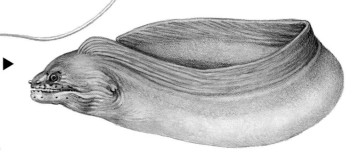

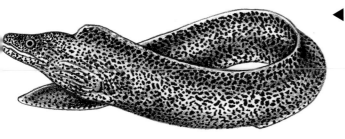

### Spotted moray eel
*Gymnothorax moringa*

A moray typical in shallow seabeds, including those with abundant vegetation, where it remains hidden in cracks during the day, coming out at night to hunt. It is yellowish white with numerous brownish or reddish black spots. Up to 3.6 feet (1 meter) in length. Common from South Carolina to Brazil.

### Goldentail moray eel
*Gymnothorax millaris*

Small moray with tapered body and small, slightly pointed head. Nocturnal, by day it takes refuge among the crevices of the coral reefs from 6 feet to more than 180 feet (54 meters) in depth. Its body is brownish, dotted with small yellow spots, its tail golden yellow, and its eyes edged with yellow. Up to 1.8 feet (.5 meters) long. Common from Florida to Brazil and around the islands of the Atlantic.

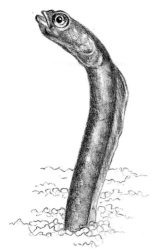

## CONGRIDAE FAMILY

### Brown garden eel
*Heteroconger halis*

Elongated grayish brown body and tapered head with large eyes and small mouth. Lives in colonies on sandy seabeds, where it always stays buried, leaving only its mouth and a portion of its body exposed. Up to 1.8 feet (.5 meters) in length. Common throughout the Caribbean.

## MEGALOPIDAE FAMILY

### Tarpon
*Megalops atlanticus*

Fish with a robust body and blunt head. Its mouth is oblique and typically upturned, its body silvery and covered with large, extremely robust scales. The last ray of its dorsal fin forms a long filament. It lives in groups that may be quite large, in shallow waters, with a preference for darker areas such as the sandy-floored canyons that are scattered throughout the Florida Keys. Up to 7.5 feet (2.25 meters) in length. Common from Virginia to Brazil.

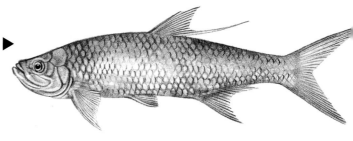

## SYNODONTIDAE FAMILY

### Sand diver
*Synodus intermedius*

Robust, elongated body, flattened ventrally. Its mouth is wide, showing its small but numerous teeth. It has a dark spot on the operculum and a series of yellowish longitudinal stripes on its flanks. Lives on sandy seafloors, where it buries itself. Up to 20 inches (50 centimeters) in length. Common from North Carolina to Brazil.

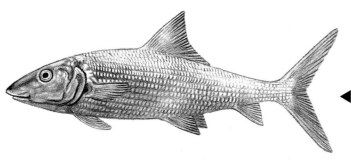

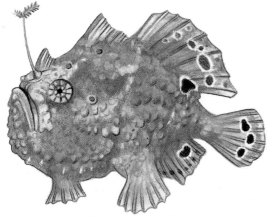

## HOLOCENTRIDAE FAMILY

### Longspine squirrelfish
*Holocentrus rufus*

Fish with an oval, compressed body with the initial part of the dorsal fin armed with robust, spiny, white-tipped rays. The second half of the dorsal fin is particularly wide. The fish is red with a white stripe below the eyes. During the day it remains hidden in the cavities of the reef; by night it goes hunting for mollusks, crustaceans, and echinoderms. Up to 11 inches (28 centimeters) in length. Common from Bermuda to Venezuela.

## ALBULIDAE FAMILY

### Bonefish
*Albula vulpes*

Fish with tapered body, pointed snout, and well-developed mouth tilted downward. The dorsal and anal fins are distinguished by a final filamentous ray. It tends to follow the tides onto sandy coastal seabeds. Lives on coralline seabeds with abundant sandy areas and in the channels of the reef, but due to its ability to use atmospheric air for respiration, it can also live in inland areas. It is silvery in color. Up to 3 feet (1 meter) in length. Common from New Brunswick to Brazil.

## ANTENNARIDAE FAMILY

### Longlure frogfish
*Antennarius multicellatus*

Fish with a wide, somewhat globular body with a wide dorsal fin and stubby ventral and pectoral fins. The first spiny ray of the dorsal fin is transformed into a long filament used to attract prey. Extremely mimetic, it will remain immobile unless it is approached too closely. It grows darker in color when frightened. The three spots on its tail are characteristic. Up to 5.5 inches (14 centimeters) in length. Common from Florida to the Caribbean.

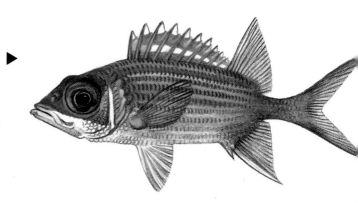

## Blackbar soldierfish
*Myripristis jacobus*

Fish with an oval body and large head and eyes. It is entirely red with the exception of a black band that covers the posterior edges of the opercula. During the day it tends to remain in caves, where it can be seen swimming upside down due to the light reflected from the seafloor. Up to 8 inches (20 centimeters) in length. Common from Georgia to Brazil as far as the Cape Verde Islands.

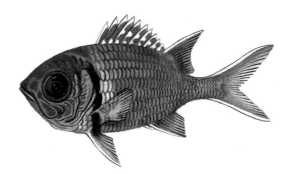

**FISTULARIDAE FAMILY**

## Bluespotted cornetfish
*Fistularia tabacaria*

Fish with an elongated body and tubular snout with terminal mouth. The two central rays of the caudal fin are quite elongated. Common near underwater meadows and reefs broken by sandy seabeds. It is solitary or lives in small groups. Up to 5.5 feet (1.65 meters) in length. Common from Nova Scotia to Brazil.

**AULOSTOMATIDAE FAMILY**

## Trumpetfish
*Aulostomus maculatus*

Fish with an elongated body and tubular snout with terminal mouth and a thin barbel under the chin. The dorsal fin is a series of distinct spiny rays. It lives near reefs, where it camouflages itself by changing color and swimming in a nearly vertical position. It is timid and not easy to approach. Up to 3 feet (1 meter) in length. Common from Florida to Brazil.

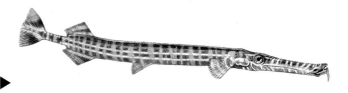

**SYNGNATHIDAE FAMILY**

## Lined seahorse
*Hippocampus erectus*

Fish with a characteristic body consisting of bony rings that support the head, located in an angular position. It is typically associated with areas with abundant vegetation, where it camouflages itself by anchoring to algae with its prehensile tail. Up to 6.5 inches (16 centimeters) in length. Common from Nova Scotia to Argentina.

**SCORPAENIDAE FAMILY**

## Spotted scorpionfish
*Scorpaena plumieri*

Scorpionfish with a robust body, with excrescences and cutaneous appendages on the snout. It is greenish brown in color, with reddish tones. The tail has three dark vertical bands, and the inner pectoral fin is black with small white spots. One of the most common scorpionfish on the reefs. Up to 16 inches (40 centimeters) in length. Common from New York to Brazil.

**DACTYLOPTERIDAE FAMILY**

## Flying gurnard
*Dactylopterus volitans*

Fish with a tapered body but stubby head, flattened at the back. Its most distinctive characteristic is the pair of large pectoral fins, with blue spots and stripes when distended. The initial rays of the ventral fins are free and mobile, so that the fish can almost walk on the sea floor. Lives on sandy or detrital seabeds and among algae. Despite its name and its large fins, it is not a flying fish. Up to 18 inches (45 centimeters) in length. Common along a large part of the Atlantic coast.

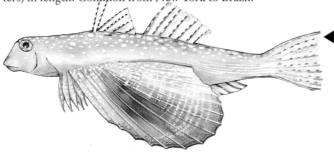

## Jewfish
*Epinephelus itajara*

This is the largest of the Atlantic groupers, with a very large, flattened head. It is greenish gray with small black spots. Tends to make its lairs in caves or sunken ships. Because of its size, it is potentially dangerous. Up to 8 feet (2.5 meters) in length. Common from Florida to Brazil, and in Africa from Senegal to the Congo.

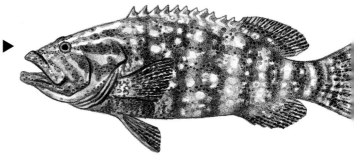

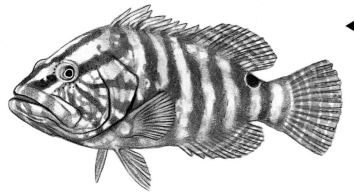

## Nassau grouper
*Epinephelus striatus*

Grouper with a tapered body and small ventral fins. Rather common on coralline seabeds, where it never ventures far from its lair. Rapidly changes its striped color if frightened or curious. During the mating season, groups of thousands of individuals gather in small areas. Up to 3 feet (1 meter) in length. Common from North Carolina to Brazil.

## Red hind
*Epinephelus guttatus*

This is considered one of the most common groupers on shallow coral reefs, where it can often be observed lying motionless on the sea floor. Its basic color is light, with red spots on the body. The edges of the dorsal, anal, and caudal fins are characteristically black. Up to 24 inches (61 centimeters) in length. Common from Florida to Brazil.

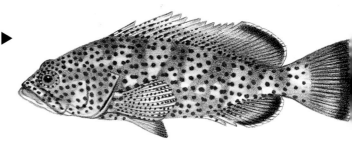

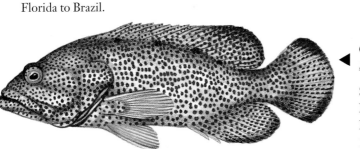

## Graysby
*Epinephelus cruentatus*

Small grouper with a tapered body and tail with rounded edge. It is light colored with numerous reddish spots all over its body. Lives on coralline seabeds, from the surface to depths of up to 120 to 210 feet (36 to 63 meters). Up to 12 inches (30 centimeters) in size. Common from Florida to Brazil.

## Coney
*Epinephelus fulvus*

Tapered body with caudal fin with a straight or slightly rounded edge, but always with well-defined angles. Its color tends to vary with the depth. It is a gregarious species and prefers reefs full of crevices, from which it rarely ventures. It can be approached slowly. Up to 16 inches (40 centimeters) in length. Common from Florida to Brazil.

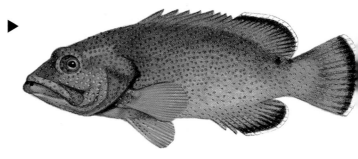

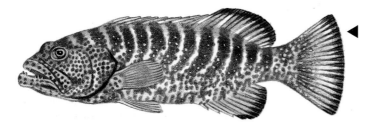

## Tiger grouper
*Mycteroperca tigris*

Grouper with a tapered body distinguished by a series of light vertical stripes on its sides, which contribute to its tiger-stripe appearance. Its basic color is reddish. Young individuals are yellow. Lives in sheltered reef areas. Up to 33 inches (84 centimeters) in size. Common from Florida to Brazil.

## Greater soapfish
*Rypticus saponaceus*

Fish with a pointed anterior profile that is straight along the back of the head. The dorsal fin is underdeveloped and has a rounded posterior edge. Lives at depths of a few yards to 150 feet (45 meters) deep, near reefs and on sandy seabeds. If frightened, it secretes a mucus toxic to other fish. Up to 13 inches (33 centimeters) in length. Common from Florida to Brazil and in the eastern Atlantic.

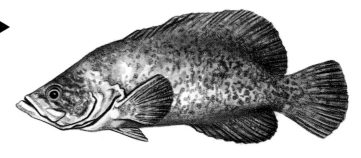

## Barred hamlet
*Hypoplectrus puella*

Fish with a compressed body and slightly pointed snout. It is brownish yellow with a dark triangular spot at the center of its flanks. Prefers rocky, shallow seabeds and coral reefs to a depth of 60 to 70 feet (18 to 21 meters). It can be approached, but is always ready to take refuge among the cracks. Up to 5 inches (13 centimeters) in length. Common from Florida to the Caribbean.

## Indigo hamlet
*Hypoplectrus indigo*

Similar to the hamlet described above, from which it can be distinguished by its bluish color with vertical white stripes. Prefers coral seabeds and lives near the seafloor. Like other species of hamlets, it can be approached slowly. Up to 5 inches (13 centimeters) in length. Common from Florida to Belize.

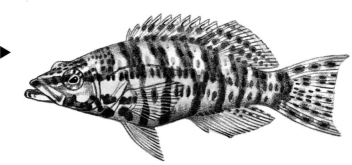

## Tobaccofish
*Serranus tabacarius*

Fish with a tapered body, distinguishable by a large, brownish orange longitudinal band. Lives near the seafloor where reefs become detrital, and near sandy seabeds. Tends to become gregarious beyond 150 feet (45 meters) in depth. Up to 7 inches (18 centimeters) in length. Common from Florida to Brazil.

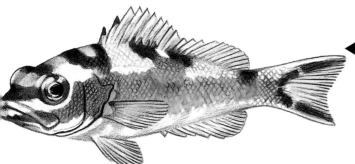

## Tigerfish
*Serranus tigrinus*

Small fish with an elongated, compressed body that terminates in a pointed snout. The opercula are spiny with toothed edges. It is tiger-striped with vertical dark bands. The tips of the lobes of the caudal fin are yellowish. Lives on coralline or meadowy seabeds. Up to 6 inches (15 centimeters) in length. Common in the Caribbean.

## Peppermint bass
*Liopropoma rubre*

Small fish with an elongated body and double dorsal fin. The tip of the dorsal, anal, and caudal fins are the same color. Its flanks are red-striped. It tends to remain hidden in crevices and caves, and for this reason is not easy to identify, despite the fact that it is common. Up to 3 inches (8 centimeters) in length. Common from Florida to Venezuela.

## Candy bass
*Liopropoma carnabi*

Small fish with tapered body and double dorsal fin. The second dorsal fin is characterized by a black spot edged in blue, which also appears on both lobes of the caudal fin. The species lives in dark crevices in the reef at depths of between 45 and 210 feet (13 and 36 meters). Up to 2.5 inches (6 centimeters) in length. Common from Florida to the Antilles.

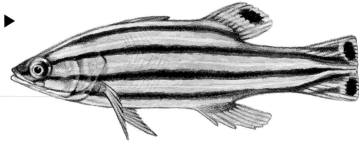

**GRAMMATIDAE FAMILY**

## Fairy basslet
*Gramma loreto*

Small fish that is quite unique due to the dual yellow and fuchsia color that divides its body in half. Lives in small groups in caves and crevices, where the effect of the light causes it to swim upside down. Up to 3 inches (8 centimeters) in length. Common from Bermuda to Venezuela.

**APOGONIDAE FAMILY**

## Flamefish
*Apogon maculatus*

Small fish with an oval, robust body and a wide caudal peduncle. Uniformly red with a black spot on the operculum and on the base of the second dorsal fin. Prefers surface waters, where it lives within caves during the day. Up to 5 inches (13 centimeters) in length. Common from Florida to the Gulf of Mexico.

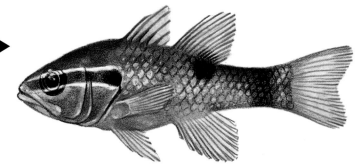

**CIRRHITIDAE FAMILY**

## Redspotted hawkfish
*Amblycirrhitus pinos*

Small fish with a wide body and pointed snout. The dorsal fin has spiny rays with fringed tips. Has small red spots on the snout, the back, and the dorsal fin. Lives on reefs, where it lies in ambush on the seafloor. Up to 4 inches (10 centimeters) long. Common from Florida to the Gulf of Mexico.

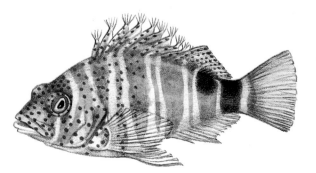

**MALACANTHIDAE FAMILY**

## Sand tilefish
*Malacanthus plumieri*

Fish with an elongated body, its terminal mouth distinguished by large lips. The caudal fin is typically crescent-shaped with pointed lobes. It is yellowish blue with yellow and bluish stripes on its head and a yellow tail. Lives on sandy and detrital seabeds, where it digs its lairs. Up to 24 inches (61 centimeters) in length. Common from North Carolina to Brazil.

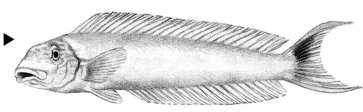

**CARANGIDAE FAMILY**

## Crevalle jack
*Caranx hippos*

Fish with an elongated, wide body, quite tapered and convex at the front. The tail is thin and typically falcate. Young individuals are gregarious and more frequent in coastal waters, while adults tend to be solitary and more common in open water or along the outer face of the reef. Up to 3 feet (1 meter) in length. Common from Nova Scotia to Uruguay and the eastern Atlantic.

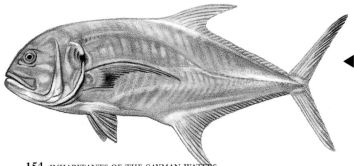

## Bar jack
*Caranx ruber*

Elongated, tapered, silvery body, distinguished by a dark band at the base of the dorsal fin that extends to the lower lobe of the caudal fin. Forms schools consisting of a variable number of individuals, and often follows schools of goatfish and stingrays to feed on the invertebrates that these fish uncover. Up to 24 inches (61 centimeters) in length. Common from New Jersey to Venezuela.

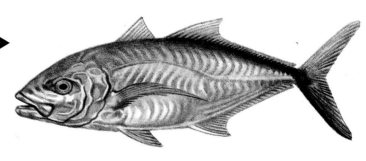

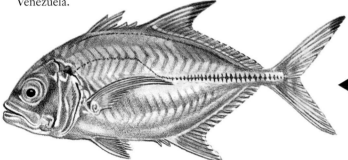

## Horse-eye jack
*Caranx latus*

Relatively wide and compressed body. Can be distinguished from other carangids by its characteristically yellow tail. Lives in schools in open water above deeper reefs, often mingling with other carangids. Up to 28 inches (71 centimeters) in length. Common from New Jersey to Brazil.

## Palometa
*Trachinotus goodei*

Carangid with a lozenge-shaped body distinguished by the well-developed rays of the dorsal and anal fins. It is silvery, with 3 to 5 black vertical stripes. Lives in coastal waters among coral formations. Up to 20 inches (51 centimeters) in size. Common from Massachusetts to Argentina.

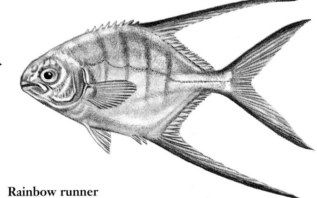

## Rainbow runner
*Elegatis bipinnulata*

Spindle-shaped, elongated fish distinguished by two light blue longitudinal bands separated by a greenish or yellowish stripe. Frequently in deep waters, it can often be found near the outer slopes of the reef. Lives in schools and is attracted by divers' bubbles. Up to 3.6 feet (1 meter) in length. Common in all circumtropical waters.

## Yellow jack
*Caranx bartholomei*

A medium-sized carangid with a tapered, compressed, but not extremely elevated body. Its eyes are large. It is light blue with silvery tones on its body, while its fins are yellow. Adults often have a black spot on the apex of the opercula. It is mostly solitary or may live in small groups along the outer reefs between the surface and 150 feet (45 meters) deep. Up to 35 inches (89 centimeters) in size. Common from Massachusetts to Brazil.

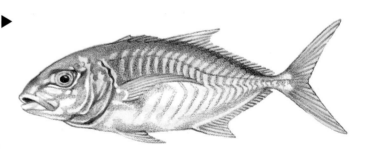

## Black jack
*Caranx lugubris*

A medium-sized jack with a tapered, compressed body and head with an inclined dorsal profile. The dorsal and anal fins are long and symmetrical. It is grayish, more or less dark, with an almost black tail and fins, a distinctive characteristic of the species. It is mostly solitary or may live in pairs in open waters, sometimes near steep slopes to depths of over 900 feet (270 meters). Up to 3 feet (1 meter) in length. Common from Florida to Brazil.

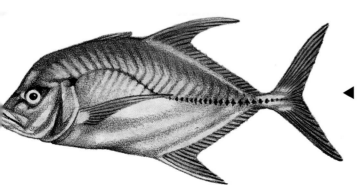

## Greater amberjack
*Seriola dumerili*

Fish with an elongated, slightly compressed body. Its eyes are small. The snout is slightly rounded. The second dorsal fin is less wide than in other carangids, but extends across most of the back. The surface of its body is smooth, with no bony shields. It is bronze-colored with a dark oblique band that covers the eyes. An amber band runs along the flanks. Lives in large schools that often frequent coastal waters to depths of more than 140 feet (42 meters). Up to 5 feet (1.5 meters) in length. Common throughout the temperate Atlantic.

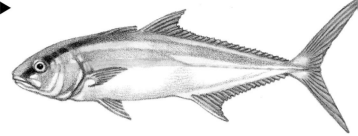

## LUTJANIDAE FAMILY

### Yellowtail snapper
*Ocyurus chrysurus*

Elongated body with extremely falcate tail and pointed lobes. Its basic color is violet blue with a longitudinal yellowish band and small spots. Lives alone or in small groups near reefs or meadows. More active at night. Up to 30 inches (76 centimeters) in length. Common from Massachusetts to Brazil.

## Mutton snapper
*Lutjanus analis*

Robust, wide, olive-colored body with a blackish stripe that is more evident in individuals up to 16 inches (40 centimeters) in length. Adults prefer rocky and coralline seabeds, while younger individuals are more common on sandy floors and meadows. Up to 30 inches (76 centimeters) in length. Common from Massachusetts to Brazil.

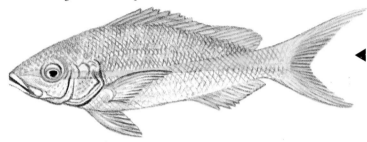

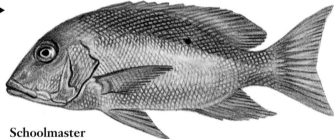

### Schoolmaster
*Lutjanus apodus*

Robust body, slightly compressed, with pointed head and well-developed mouth. Its color varies from silvery to bronze. The yellow fins and blue stripes on the snout are characteristic. Lives in groups of a few dozen individuals, usually remaining a short distance from the seafloor in areas with abundant gorgonians and large corals, at depths of between 6 and 90 feet (1.8 and 27 meters). Up to 24 inches (61 centimeters) in length. Common throughout the Caribbean and along the temperate coasts of the American continent.

## Gray snapper
*Lutjanus griseus*

Robust, slightly compressed body with pointed head and well-developed mouth. Its color varies from more or less dark gray to reddish. It has no particularly distinctive features except for a dark band, not always visible, which masks the eyes and extends from the mouth to the beginning of the dorsal fin. Lives in small schools that commonly frequent coastal waters and mangrove forests as well as reefs, from the surface to 75 feet (22 meters) deep. Up to 24 inches (61 centimeters) in size. Common from Massachusetts to Brazil.

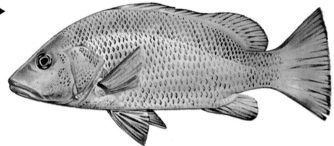

## HEMULIDAE FAMILY

### Bluestriped grunt
*Haemulon sciurus*

Wide, compressed body characterized by the dark color of the back half of the dorsal fin and the caudal fin. Its basic color is yellowish, with numerous longitudinal blue stripes. Forms large schools near the coast, on rocky or sandy seabeds. Up to 18 inches (46 centimeters) in length. Common from South Carolina to Brazil.

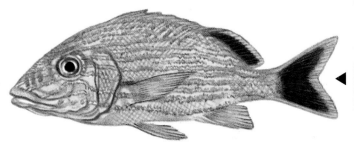

## French grunt
*Haemulon flavolineatum*

Wide body with pointed snout and small mouth. Yellowish, with numerous horizontal blue stripes above the lateral line, and oblique stripes below it. Prefers coralline seabeds, where it gathers in schools that may consist of up to a thousand individuals. Prefers darker areas. Up to 12 inches (30 centimeters) in length. Common from South Carolina to Brazil.

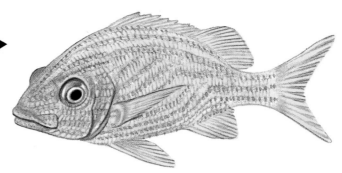

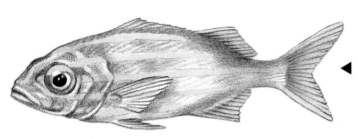

## White grunt
*Haelmulon plumieri*

Tapered, fairly wide body with robust head and slightly concave dorsal profile. It is bluish silver or yellow in color, with blue stripes on the head only. Lives in large schools near the seafloor close to large colonies of acropora corals on reefs from 6 to 60 feet (2 to 18 meters) deep. Sometimes two individuals may demonstrate territorial behavior by swimming mouth to mouth. Up to 18 inches (45 centimeters) in length. Common from Maryland to Brazil.

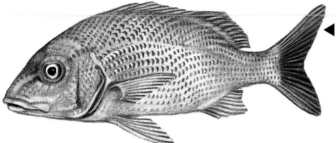

## SCIAENIDAE FAMILY

## Jack-knife fish
*Equetus lanceolatus*

Fish with a body wide at the front and quite pointed at the back. The very wide first dorsal fin is characteristic, especially in young individuals. It has a distinctive dark band that extends from the apex of the dorsal fin to the caudal fin. Prefers the darker areas of reefs and caves. Up to 10 inches (25 centimeters) in length. Common from South Carolina to Brazil.

## Smallmouth grunt
*Haemulon chrysargyreum*

Tapered, slightly compressed body with small head and large eyes. It is silvery white, with five to six horizontal yellow stripes on its flanks. Its fins are yellow. It lives in schools near the seafloor in proximity to large coral formations on reefs 6 to 54 feet (2 to 16 meters) deep, where wave action is more pronounced. Up to 9 inches (23 centimeters) in size. Common from Florida to Brazil.

## White margate
*Haemulon album*

Compressed body with wide upper profile. Its color is grayish and not very noticeable, sometimes interrupted by three dark stripes on the flanks. The caudal fin is blackish. It lives in extremely varied environments: phanerogam meadows, sandy seabeds and coral reefs at depths of from 6 to 60 feet (2 to 18 meters). Lives isolated in small groups. Measures up to 24 inches (61 centimeters) in length and is the largest of the Caribbean grunts. Common from Florida to Brazil.

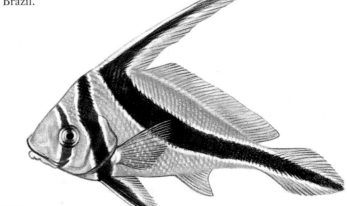

## Highhat
*Pareques acuminatus*

Body wide yet stubby in the anterior portion, with an evident dorsal fin that is nevertheless not very wide. It is reddish brown with whitish longitudinal stripes. Prefers surface waters near rocky and coralline seabeds near caves and poorly illuminated areas. Up to 9 inches (23 centimeters) in length. Common from South Carolina to Brazil.

## Spotted drum
*Equetus punctatus*

▶

Small fish with compressed body, well-developed head, and tapered posterior portion. The very wide, falcate initial rays of the dorsal fin are characteristic. The caudal fin is lozenge-shaped. Its basic coloring is white, with wide dark oblique bands on the head that gradually become horizontal along the flanks. The second half of the dorsal, caudal, and anal fins are dark and spotted with white. Mostly solitary and nocturnal, living on coralline seabeds at depths of between 9 and 90 feet (3 and 27 meters), sheltered in caves. Up to 10 inches (25 centimeters) in length. Common from Florida to Brazil.

## Spotted goatfish
*Pseudopeneus maculatus*

Tapered body with slightly pointed snout. The edge of the operculum has a more or less evident spine. It is distinguished by three large black spots on its flanks. It hunts in small groups of four to six individuals. Lives in groups on sandy seabeds near the reef, to a depth of about 150 feet (45 meters). Up to 10 inches (25 centimeters) in length. Common from Florida to Brazil.

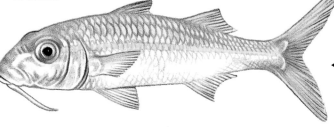

### MULLIDAE FAMILY

## Yellow goatfish
*Mulloidichthys martinicus*

◀

Tapered body with snout with a slightly convex and pointed edge. Olive-colored on the back and lighter on the sides, where there is a yellow longitudinal band extending to the tail. Forms small groups on sandy seabeds near reefs or within lagoons from just a few yards to 150 feet (45 meters) deep. Up to 16 inches (41 centimeters) in length. Common from the Caribbean to Cape Verde.

▶

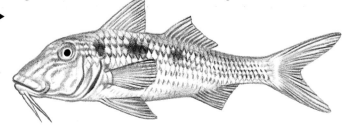

### PEMPHERIDAE FAMILY

## Glassy sweeper
*Pempheris schomburgki*

Small fish with oval body, compressed and tapered to the back. The black-edged anal fin is quite long. The fish is silvery pink in color. It is nocturnal. During the day it lives in schools within caves or in cracks in the reef, at depths of between 9 and 90 feet (3 and 27 meters). Up to 6 inches (15 centimeters) in length. Common from Florida to Brazil.

◀

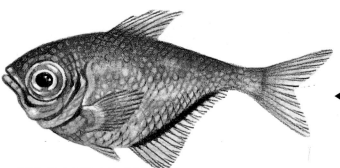

### KYPHOSIDAE FAMILY

## Bermuda chub
*Kyphosus sectatrix*

Wide, oval body with small, terminal mouth. Grayish in color with narrow, bronze-colored longitudinal stripes. Tends to form schools near coral and rocky seabeds with abundant algae, to depths of up to 90 feet (27 meters). Up to 30 inches (76 centimeters) in length. Common from Massachusetts to Brazil.

▶

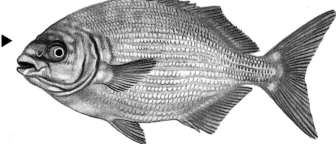

### EPHIPPIDAE FAMILY

## Atlantic spadefish
*Chaetodipterus faber*

◀

Very wide, compressed body with lobes of the dorsal and anal fins extending out to the back. It is grayish in color, with four to five dark vertical bands. Gathers in schools with as many as 500 individuals. Prefers open waters between 9 and 75 feet (3 and 22 meters) deep . Sometimes it will spontaneously approach divers. Up to 36 inches (91 centimeters) in length. Common from Massachusetts to Brazil.

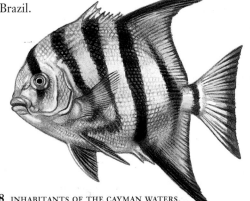

# CHETODONTIDAE FAMILY

### Foureye butterflyfish ▶
*Chaetodon capistratus*

Butterflyfish with a wide, compressed body and pointed snout. Silvery in color, shading into yellow on the belly. The large ocellar spot on the caudal peduncle is characteristic. One of the most common butterflyfish in the Caribbean. Lives in pairs around the tops of stony corals, at depths of between 6 and 60 feet (2 and 18 meters). Up to 6 inches (15 centimeters) in length. Common from New England to Panama.

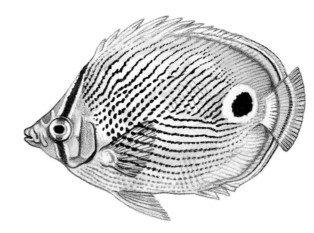

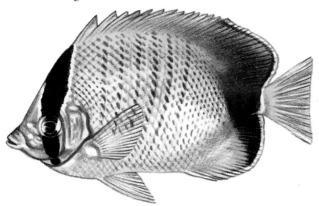

### ◀ Reef butterflyfish
*Chaetodon sedentarius*

Fish with a wide, compressed body with an almost vertical posterior profile. It is yellowish in color and has a wide, dark band extending back from the dorsal fin to the anal fin. Prefers coralline sea beds, where it lives to depths of 240 to 270 feet (72 to 81 meters). Up to 6 inches (15 centimeters) in length. Common from North Carolina to Brazil.

### Spotfin butterflyfish ▶
*Chaetodon ocellatus*

Fish with a wide, compressed body characterized by yellow fins and a small black spot on the posterior edge of the dorsal fin. At night it tends to grow darker in color. Generally lives in pairs near reefs and rocky sea beds at about 9 to 90 feet (3 to 27 meters) in depth. Up to 8 inches (20 centimeters) in length. Common from Massachusetts to Brazil.

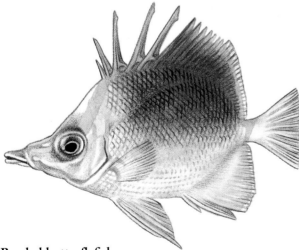

### ◀ Longsnout butterflyfish
*Chaetodon aculeatus*

Fish with very wide body due to the dorsal fin, which has more developed spiny rays. Its snout is long and pointed. Tends to be solitary and prefers deeper coralline seabeds (up to 270 feet [81 meters] in depth) and cracks in the reef, where it takes shelter if frightened. Up to 4 inches (10 centimeters) in length. Common from Florida to Venezuela.

### Banded butterflyfish
*Chaetodon striatus* ▶

Wide, compressed, whitish body with three dark, oblique bands, the first of which masks the eyes. Young individuals have an ocellar spot on the caudal peduncle. It may be either solitary or live in pairs near corals at depths of between 9 and 60 feet (3 and 18 meters). May form hybrid species with spotfin butterflyfish. Up to 6 inches (15 centimeters) in length. Common from Massachusetts to Brazil.

# POMACANTHIDAE FAMILY

**Gray angelfish**

*Pomacanthus arcuatus*

Angelfish with wide, compressed body with pointed posterior lobes of the dorsal fin and caudal fin. The caudal fin has a straight posterior edge. It is grayish brown with a very light-colored mouth. It is solitary or lives in pairs in the richest areas of the reef, at depths of between 20 and 270 feet (6 and 90 meters). Up to 20 inches (50 centimeters) in length. Common from Bermuda to Brazil.

**Rock beauty**

*Holacanthus tricolor*

Butterflyfish with a distinctive color: its front portion and tail are yellow, its midsection is black, and its mouth is blue. The lobes of the dorsal, anal, and caudal fins are pointed. It is quite territorial and tends to remain near its area of the reef, on seabeds that may reach 270 feet (81 meters) in depth. Up to 8 inches (20 centimeters) long. Common from Georgia to Brazil.

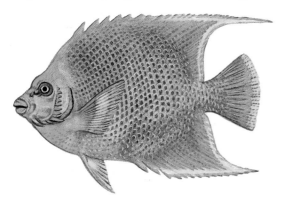

**Queen angelfish**

*Holacanthus ciliaris*

Angelfish with wide, compressed body with very pointed lobes of the dorsal and anal fins, extending beyond the edge of the caudal fin. It is yellow, with dense blue spots on the flanks and a blue spot on the head. Lives both in shallower waters of the reef as well as at greater depths (beyond 150 feet [45 meters]). Up to 18 inches (45 centimeters) in length. Common from Bermuda to Brazil.

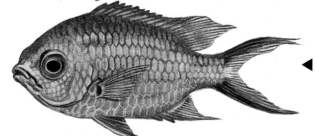

**French angelfish**

*Pomacanthus paru*

Angelfish with a rounded, compressed body with pointed, extended posterior lobes of the dorsal and anal fins. It is blackish with yellow spots on the snout and pectoral fins. It prefers surface areas of the reef with abundant gorgonians, although it can be found down to depths of about 300 feet (90 meters). Up to 12 inches (28 centimeters) in length. Common from Florida to Brazil.

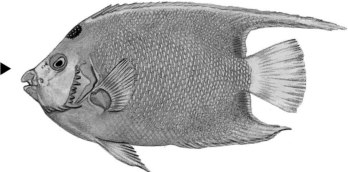

**Blue angelfish**

*Holacanthus bermudensis*

Angelfish with a wide, compressed body with very pointed lobes of the dorsal and anal fins, which extend back to beyond the edge of the caudal fin. It is blue, with yellow-edged fins. Seems to prefer more surface areas of the reefs, although it has often been observed at depths of over 240 feet (72 meters). Up to 15 inches (38 centimeters) in length. Common from Florida to the Yucatan.

# POMACENTRIDAE FAMILY

**Blue chromis**

*Chromis cyanea*

Small fish with oval body and deeply indented caudal fin. It is bluish in color, with a black-edged back and lobes of the caudal fin. It is fairly common in the waters above reefs, where it gathers in schools that may live to depths of 150 feet (45 meters). Up to 5 inches (13 centimeters) in length. Common from Florida to Venezuela.

## Brown chromis
*Chromis multilineata*

Chromis with an olive gray body distinguished by a black spot at the base of the pectoral fins, with the edges of the back and tips of the caudal fin yellow. Lives in groups above coral formations as does *Chromis cyanea*, but at shallower depths. Up to 6.5 inches (16.5 centimeters) in length. Common from Florida to Brazil.

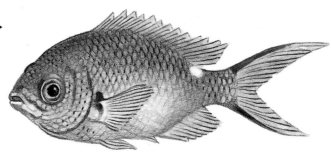

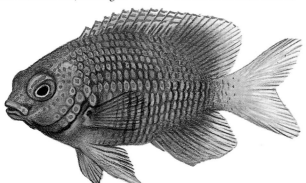

## Beaugregory
*Stegastes leucostictos*

Small fish, somewhat oval in shape, with a forked tail and rounded lobes. It is brownish, with a lighter or yellowish tail. It is a territorial species and prefers sandy and detrital seabeds with abundant algae, where it colonizes portions of the shallower parts of the seabed, 3 to 15 feet (1 to 5 meters) in depth. Up to 4 inches (10 centimeters) in length. Common from Maine to Brazil.

## Bicolor damselfish
*Stegastes partitus*

Small fish with a compressed, oval body and small terminal mouth. The anterior portion of the body is dark, while the posterior area is white. Lives between the surface to 140 feet deep (42 meters), near meadows and algae or along the reef, where it establishes territories that it defends from other members of the species. Up to 5 inches (13 centimeters) in length. Common from Florida to the Gulf of Mexico.

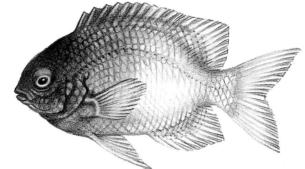

## Three-spot damselfish
*Stegastes planifrons*

Small fish with compressed, oval body with small terminal mouth. It is dark, with eyes edged in yellow and black spots at the base of the pectoral fin and on the caudal fin. Lives at depths of between 3 and 90 feet (1 and 27 meters) and prefers more illuminated surface areas of the reef with abundant algae, where it establishes territories that it tenaciously defends, even from divers. Up to 5 inches (13 centimeters) in length. Common from Florida to the Gulf of Mexico.

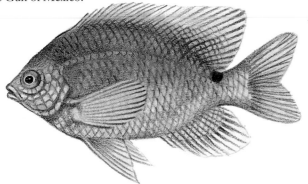

## Sergeant major
*Abdudefduf saxatilis*

Fish with a compressed, ovoid, wide body with rough scales that cover even the fins. It is whitish silver in color, with dark vertical bands and a yellowish band on the base on the dorsal fin. Lives in schools in the upper parts of the reef between 3 and 36 feet (1 and 11 meters) in depth. Up to 8 inches (20 centimeters) long. Common from Rhode Island to Uruguay.

## Yellowtail damselfish
*Microspatodon chrysurus*

Small fish with a robust, brownish body with small bluish spots and a characteristically yellow tail. Young individuals tend to remain among the branches of fire corals and may act as cleaner fish. Adults occupy small territories in the upper portions of the reef, between the surface and 45 feet (15 meters) in depth. Up to 8 inches (20 centimeters) long. Common from Florida to Venezuela.

## Cocoa damselfish
*Stegastes variabilis*

Oval body with pointed snout and slightly indented caudal fin. The dorsal fin is well developed. It is olive brown on the back and tends to become yellowish on the belly. Young individuals are blue in the dorsal area, with a black spot on the dorsal fin and one on the caudal peduncle. Lives near coral reefs between the surface and a depth of 100 feet (30 meters). Establishes territories on the seabed that it fiercely defends, especially during the mating season. Up to 5 inches (13 centimeters) in length. Common from Florida to Brazil.

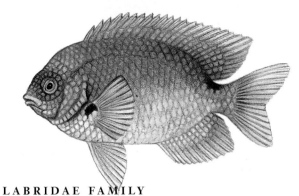

## Creole wrasse
*Clepticus parrae*

Large wrasse with tapered body. The lobes of the dorsal and anal fins are pointed. The tail is slightly sickle-shaped. Adults are violet in color, with the posterior portion of the body yellowish. The mouth is light-colored. Prefers the deeper parts of the reef, to a depth of 120 feet (36 meters), where it forms large schools prior to sunset. Up to 12 inches (30 centimeters) in length. Common from North Carolina to the Gulf of Mexico.

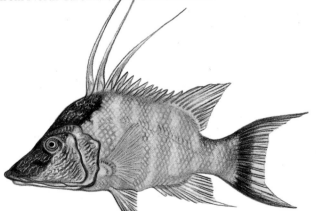

## Bluehead wrasse
*Thalassoma bifasciatum*

Elongated, compressed body. Its color is quite variable, depending on age. In adults, the posterior portion of the body is greenish, with the anterior portion bluish with intermediate white and black stripes. Young individuals are yellowish in color. Lives in a wide variety of environments between the surface and 120 feet (36 meters) deep. Up to 7 inches (18 centimeters) in length. Common from Florida to Venezuela.

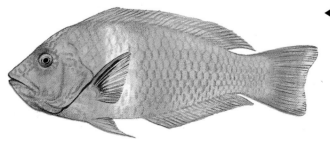

**LABRIDAE FAMILY**

## Spanish hogfish
*Bodianus rufus*

Fish with a robust body and pointed head. The dorsal area is purple, with the rest of the body yellowish in color. It swims continuously near coralline seabeds between the surface and 594 feet (180 meters) deep. It will approach divers confidently. Up to 16 inches (40 centimeters) in length. Common from Florida to Brazil.

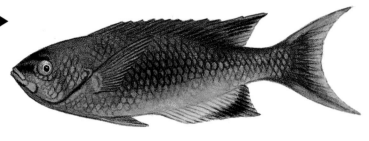

## Hogfish
*Lachnolaimus maximus*

Rather large wrasse with pointed head. It is recognizable primarily by the particularly well developed initial rays of the dorsal fin. It is whitish in color, with a dark dorsal band extending from the snout to the tail. Prefers sandy seabeds, including those along the outer slope of the reef to depths of 90 feet (27 meters), where it digs in search of prey. Up to 35 inches (89 centimeters) in length. Common from North Carolina to Brazil.

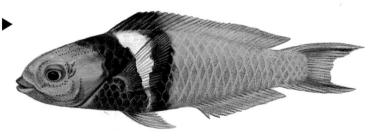

## Puddingwife
*Halichoeres radiatus*

Particularly wide body, bluish or greenish in color, with a yellow-edged caudal fin. It is difficult to approach due to the fact that it is constantly in motion and extremely suspicious. Lives on coralline seabeds and mixed coralline and detrital beds to a depth of about 120 feet (36 meters). Up to 20 inches (51 centimeters) in length. Found from North Carolina to Brazil.

## Slippery dick
*Halichoeres bivittatis*

Wrasse with a tapered, wide body and a broad caudal fin. Its color varies widely, but is usually greenish. A dark longitudinal band runs along the center of the flanks. The tips of the lobes of the caudal fin are dark. It lives in varied habitats, from coralline to sandy areas as well as meadows in surface waters, 3 to 45 feet (1 to 13 meters) deep. Up to 10 inches (25 centimeters) in length. Common from North Carolina to Brazil.

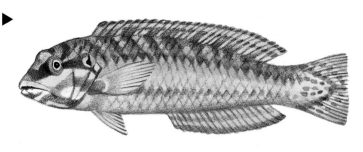

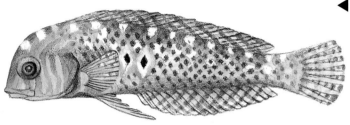

## SCARIDAE FAMILY

## Blue parrotfish
*Scarus coeruleus*

Tapered, robust body. Adult males have a distinctive frontal swelling that alters the anterior profile of the snout. It is mostly bluish in color. It feeds primarily on algae, and thus actively moves from one area of the reef to another, to depths of 75 feet (22.5 meters). Up to 35 inches (89 centimeters) in length. Common from Maryland to Brazil.

## Green razorfish
*Xyrichtys splendens*

Fish with a wide, very compressed body, rounded snout, and oblique profile. Greenish in color, with a small dark lateral spot (typical of males) and eyes with a red iris. Tends to remain nearly immobile near seabeds with meadows or on sandy floors with gorgonians, at depths of between 9 and 45 feet (3 and 13 meters). If threatened, it buries itself in the sediments. Up to 6 inches (15 centimeters) in length. Common from Florida to Brazil.

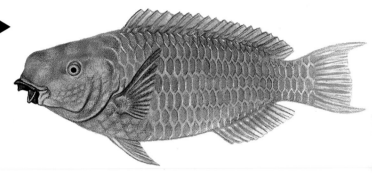

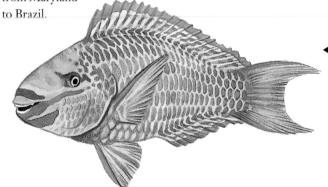

## Queen parrotfish
*Scarus vetula*

Greenish blue parrotfish with scales edged in orange-pink. The snout has wide blue stripes around the mouth and near the eye. Frequents coral reefs to depths of 250 feet (75 meters). Up to 24 inches (61 centimeters) in length. Common from Florida to Argentina.

## Stoplight parrotfish
*Sparisoma viride*

Parrotfish that is primarily green in color, with oblique pink-orange bands on the head and caudal fin and a yellow spot on the operculum. It is a rather common species between 9 and 150 feet (3 and 45 meters) in depth, especially where the coralline sea beds are separated by areas with abundant vegetation. Up to 20 inches (51 centimeters) in length. Common from Florida to Brazil.

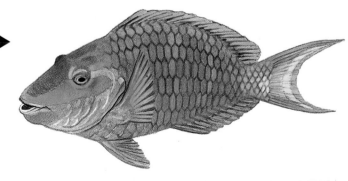

## Redband parrotfish
*Sparisoma aurofrenatum*

Parrotfish that is greenish in color with shades of orange and pink. There is an orange band along the sides of the mouth. The fins have purple tones. Prefers reefs with abundant algae and coralline and rocky seabeds to a depth of 60 feet (18 meters). Up to 14 inches (35 centimeters) in length. Common from Florida to Brazil.

## Princess parrotfish
*Scarus taeniopterus*

Small, greenish blue parrotfish with a yellow lateral band and blue stripes on the snout. The caudal and dorsal fins have distinctively colored edges: yellow, orange, or pink. Adults live in small groups, while young and immature individuals are much more gregarious. Prefers rocky coastal areas and outer reefs, to a depth of 247 feet (75 meters). Up to 14 inches (35 centimeters) in length. Common from Florida to Brazil.

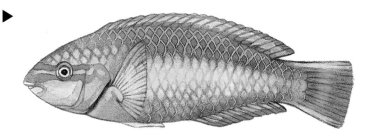

### SPHYRAENIDAE FAMILY

## Great barracuda
*Sphyraena barracuda*

Elongated, subcylindrical body with long, pointed snout and prominent lower jaw. The two dorsal fins are clearly separated. The caudal fin is slightly crescent-shaped, with pointed lobes. It is silvery in color, with dark vertical bands and small posterior spots. Lives in coastal waters and above coralline or sandy seabeds or meadows. Up to 6 feet (2 meters) in length. Common in all circumtropical waters.

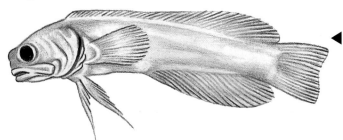

### GOBIDAE FAMILY

## Neon goby
*Gobiosoma oceanops*

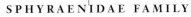

Small goby easily recognizable by its dark color, with two longitudinal fluorescent blue stripes. Acts as a cleaner fish, and gathers in groups at typical "service stations." Lives on coralline seabeds near large stony corals between 9 and 130 feet (3 and 39 meters) in depth. Up to 2 inches (5 centimeters) in length. Common from Florida to the Honduras.

### OPISTOGNATHIDAE FAMILY

## Yellowhead jawfish
*Opistognathus aurifrons*

A small benthic fish with an elongated, tapered body that ends in a short but robust head with large eyes. It is blue with a yellowish head. Usually lives on the seabed at depths of between 9 and 120 feet (3 and 36 meters), where it digs lairs in which it will rapidly take refuge. Up to 4 inches (10 centimeters) in length. Common from Florida to Venezuela.

### BLENNIDAE FAMILY

## Redlip blenny
*Ophioblennius atlanticus*

Blenny with a compressed body and obtuse snout. The mouth is distinguished by large lips. It is dark in color with pectoral and caudal fins tinged with yellow or red. It is territorial and prefers rocky seabeds and the upper areas of the reef. Up to 5 inches (13 centimeters) in length. Common from North Carolina to Brazil.

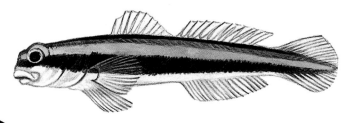

## Yellowline goby
*Gobiosoma horsti*

Small goby easily recognizable by the dark color of its back, where a yellow longitudinal stripe runs from the eye to the tail. Usually lives between 20 and 80 feet (6 and 24 meters) in depth near sponges, where it dwells within the larger pores of tubular sponges. Up to 1.5 inches (4 centimeters) in length. Common from Florida to the Antilles.

# ACANTHURIDAE FAMILY

### Surgeonfish
*Acanthurus chirurgus*

A wide, compressed, brownish body distinguished by a series of dark vertical stripes that may or may not be visible. In general this is a solitary species, although it may live with other surgeonfish near coral reefs and rocky shoals at depths of between 9 and 60 feet (3 and 18 meters). Up to 10 inches (25 centimeters) in length. Common from Massachusetts to Brazil.

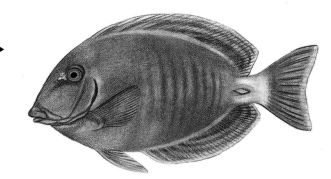

### Blue tang
*Acanthurus coeruleus*

Surgeonfish that is bluish in color, with lighter fins. The cutting laminae typical of surgeonfish can be seen on the caudal peduncle. If frightened, it can change color rapidly. It tends to be solitary, but may gather in dense schools, mingling with other surgeonfish. Up to 9 inches (23 centimeters) in length. Common from Bermuda to Brazil.

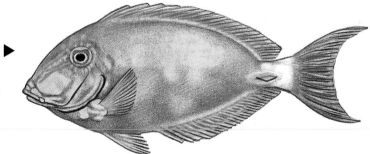

### Bahia surgeonfish
*Acanthurus bahianus*

Surgeonfish with coloring varying from blue-gray to dark brown. Light-colored spokes surround the eyes. Prefers flat or slightly-sloping coral seabeds. Measures up to 14 inches (35 centimeters). Found from Massachusetts to Brazil.

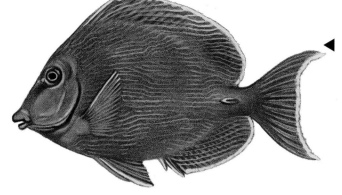

# BOTHIDAE FAMILY

### Peacock flounder
*Bothus lunatus*

Flounder characterized by a series of ocellar spots on the body and small bluish spots on the fins. The pectoral fin is quite elongated and is often held erect. Lives from depths of 3 to 300 feet (1 to 90 meters) on seabeds with meadows and sandy or detrital floors among corals or at the edges of mangrove forests, where it camouflages itself through its ability to change color. Up to 16 inches (40 centimeters) in length. Common from Florida to Brazil.

# BALISTIDAE FAMILY

### Queen triggerfish
*Balistes vetula*

Triggerfish that has dorsal and caudal fins with elongated and pointed lobes. It is characterized by a pair of blue stripes on the snout and blue stripes on the odd-numbered fins. Lives on coralline seabeds broken by wide sandy and detrital areas, at depths of from 6 to over 150 feet (2 to 45 meters). Up to 24 inches (61 centimeters) in length. Common from Massachusetts to Brazil.

## Black durgon
*Melichthys niger*

Triggerfish with a blackish body and bluish white stripes on the base of the dorsal and anal fins. Lives in small groups that remain near the seabed or in open waters near the outer slope of the reef, at depths of between 15 and 180 feet (5 and 54 meters). Up to 20 inches (51 centimeters) in length. Common from Florida to Brazil and in circumtropical waters.

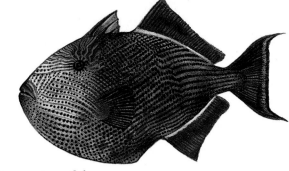

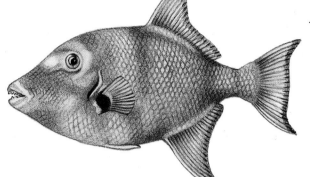

## MONOCANTHIDAE FAMILY

## Scrawled filefish
*Aluterus scriptus*

Fish with a tapered body, pointed snout and enlarged tail. It has irregular stripes and small blue spots. It is solitary and lives in lagoons and along the outer slopes of the reef, from which it travels to open waters. Up to 3 feet (1 meter) in length. Common in circumtropical waters.

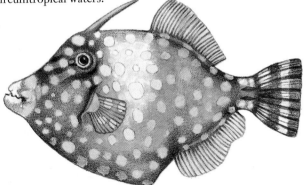

## OSTRACIIDAE FAMILY

## Smooth trunkfish
*Lactophyrys triqueter*

Fish with triangular body with large hexagonal bony plaques. It is dark-colored, with numerous light spots. It is normally solitary, but may gather in small groups. Prefers coralline seabeds mixed with sandy areas at depths of between 10 and 75 feet (3 to 22.5 meters). Up to 12 inches (30 centimeters) in length. Common from Massachusetts to Brazil.

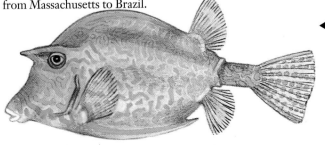

## Ocean triggerfish
*Canthidermis sufflamen*

Triggerfish with a wide, oval body with pointed, falcate dorsal and anal fins. It is uniformly gray in color, with a black spot at the base of the pectoral fins. It is solitary or lives in small groups in open waters near reefs and coral slopes at depths of between 25 and 120 feet (7.5 and 36 meters). During the mating season it moves to sandy seabeds. Up to 25.5 inches (65 centimeters) in length. Common from Florida to Argentina to the Cape Verde Islands.

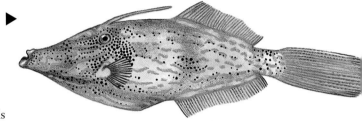

## Whitespotted filefish
*Cantherines macrocerus*

Fish with a somewhat oval body with a ventral edge that has an evident bulge in front of the anal fin. The snout is slightly pointed, with a more developed lower jaw. It is olive gray dorsally and orange brown ventrally. It may or may not have white spots. There are orange spines on the caudal peduncle. Lives in pairs in lagoons or near reefs with abundant gorgonians, at depths of between 15 and 75 feet (4.5 and 22.5 meters). Up to 16.5 inches (42 centimeters) long. Common from Florida to Brazil.

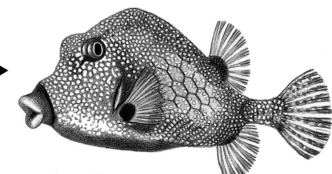

## Scrawled cowfish
*Lactophyrys quadricornis*

Fish with triangular body with a long caudal peduncle and two spines above the eyes. It is yellowish in color, with numerous blue spots and stripes. It is usually solitary and lives at depths of between 6 and 75 feet (2 and 22.5 meters), with a preference for coralline seabeds and meadows, where it camouflages itself by changing color. Up to 19 inches (48 centimeters) in length. Common from Massachusetts to Brazil.

## Spotted trunkfish
*Lactophyrys bicaudalis*

Fish with a nearly polygonal body with two robust anterior spines on the anal fin. It is white with black spots, which appear on the fins as well. The mouth is white. It is solitary or lives in small groups at depths of between 10 and 75 feet (3 and 22.5 meters), on coralline seabeds mixed with sandy areas. Up to 18 inches (46 centimeters) in length. Common from Florida to Brazil.

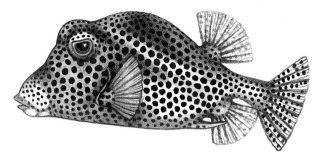

## Chequered puffer
*Sphoeroides testudineus*

Rounded, spindle-shaped body distinguished by light geometric lines that form a sort of network. Prefers coastal bays, rocky formations, and meadows between the surface and about 180 feet (54 meters) in depth. It is not frequent near reefs. Up to 12 inches (30 centimeters) in length. Common from Bermuda to Brazil.

## TETRAODONTIDAE FAMILY

## Bandtailed puffer
*Sphoeroides spengleri*

Elongated body, rounded at the front. The large nostrils can easily be seen on the head. It has a series of horizontally positioned spots along the flanks below the lateral line. Almost always lives near the seabed, on meadows or coralline or detrital areas at depths of between 6 and 90 feet (2 and 27 meters). Up to 7 inches (18 centimeters) in length. Common from Massachusetts to Brazil.

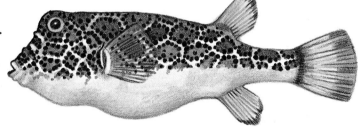

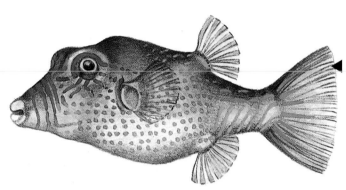

## DIODONTHIDAE FAMILY

## Burrfish
*Diodon hystrix*

Tapered yet thickened and rounded body in the anterior portion. Its eyes are bulging. The mouth has a single dental plate for each jaw. The epidermis is dotted with spines that rise when the animal swells. During the day it tends to remain in caves or in other darker areas of the reef, at depths of between 6 and 75 feet (2 and 22.5 meters). Up to 35 inches (89 centimeters) in length. Common from Massachusetts to Brazil and in all circumtropical waters.

## Longnose puffer
*Canthigaster rostrata*

Small puffer with an especially pointed snout and a small, terminal mouth. It is dark-colored on the back and yellowish on the flanks. There are blue stripes and spots around the eyes, near the mouth and on the tail. Prefers coralline seabeds and meadows at depths of between 3 and 90 feet (1 and 27 meters). Up to 4 inches (10 centimeters) in length. Common from Florida to Venezuela.

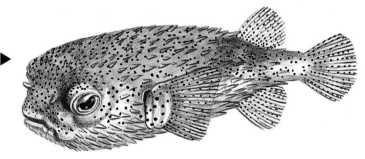

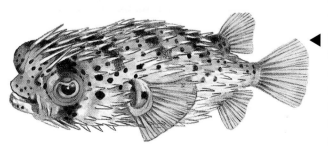

## Balloonfish
*Diodon holacanthus*

Stubby, oval, and lightly depressed body with spines. Those on the head are rather long. If attacked, it swells, raising its spines in defense. It is olive or brownish in color, with small dark spots that are not present on the fins. Lives at depths of between 6 and 75 feet (2 and 22.5 meters), in lagoons, reefs with corals mixed with detrital areas, and phanerogam meadows. Up to 19 inches (48 centimeters) in length. Common from Florida to Brazil and in many circumtropical areas.

*Many Cayman reefs are suitable for snorkeling, with healthy coral formations in shallow water.*

*The authors wish to express their gratitude for the diving services provided by Sunset House, Red Sail Sports, Parrots Landing, and Treasure Island Divers on Grand Cayman, as well as Divi Tiara Beach Resort for the access they provided to dive sites on Cayman Brac and Little Cayman. Bill Brock of Sunset Divers provided Grand Cayman dive site reference maps, and the materials for Cayman Brac and Little Cayman maps were courtesy Shawn Lunt of Divi Tiara.*

*Slide film processing for the photographs used in this book was courtesy of Stephen Frink Photographic, and stock photography management was provided by WaterHouse Stock Photography, both located in Key Largo, Florida.*

**Text and photographs:** *Stephen Frink and William Harrigan*
**Illustrators:** *Cristina Franco (dive sites); Monica Falcone ("Inhabitants of the Cayman Waters")*
**Editors:** *Valeria Manferto De Fabianis and Laura Accomazzo*
**Production editor:** *Abigail Asher*
**Text designer:** *Barbara Balch*
**Cover designer:** *Paula Winicur*